Crooked
TREE

*To Jackie
From Susan
with love
April 2015*

Crooked TREE

A Memoir of Faith

REBECCA BIEGERT CONTI

All Scripture quotations, unless otherwise indicated, are taken from The Holy Bible, New International Version, NIV. Copyright 1973, 1978, 1984.

Copyright © 2014 Rebecca Biegert Conti
All rights reserved.

Cover art by Roberta Rogers

ISBN: 150107783X
ISBN 13: 9781501077838

For

Shauna, Natalie,

Marcus and Preston

Table of Contents

Crooked Tree · xi
Preface · xiii
First Awareness · 1
Joy on a Swing Set · 3
Glimpses of Childhood · 7
Surrender · 11
First Steps · 15
A Christmas Poem · 19
For Brad · 21
The End of a Short Life · 23
Grief: The Vacuum We Inhabit · 27
Family Life · 31
Rupture · 35
The Hardest of the Hard Years · 37
Veil · 43
An Unexpected Gift · 45
Into the Miracles Jar · 49
Seminary: A Dream Realized · 51
Under Heaven · 53
Dating · 57
Grand Canyon at 115 Degrees · 59
Bath · 61
Aching Loneliness · 63
A Strange Prayer · 65
Praise Man · 67
Awkward Phone Call aka Daughter Freaks Out · 69

Timing Is Everything · 71
New Chapter · 73
Healing · 75
Land of the Living · 79
A(nother) True Story · 81
Scattered Loved Ones · 83
Serving God Together · 85
What Has Come to Pass · 87
An Old Friend · 89
Uncle Barney and Black-eyed Peas · · · · · · · · · · · · · · · 91
When Our Pain Blesses Others · · · · · · · · · · · · · · · · · · 93
To Our Doorstep · 95
His Nearness · 97
Hi Y'all · 99
Running · 101
Life and Death · 103
Prayer for Protection · 105
Hidden Hollow Prayer Chapel · · · · · · · · · · · · · · · · · · 109
Heartache · 111
Memorial Service for Weston Max · · · · · · · · · · · · · · 113
Sad · 117
Joy and Heartache Side by Side · · · · · · · · · · · · · · · · · 119
Fresh Rosemary and a Thorn · · · · · · · · · · · · · · · · · · 121
Be Still · 123
How to Think · 125
Weaning · 127
Seasons · 129
Home · 131
Abundance · 133
Morning · 135

Appendix

Remembering Theo	141
Hidden Hollow Prayer Chapel Dedication	149
A Contemplation of the Table of Grace	151
The Upside-Down Kingdom	155
Life, Death, Burial & Resurrection	163
The Silent Measure	169
Acknowledgements	173
About the Author	175

Crooked Tree

                                        Majestic

                              Crooked

                Old, perhaps ancient

        Sunlit peaks beyond

                My life lived in its shadow

                            Its life

                            An icon

                                              Hidden Hollow
                                                June, 2014

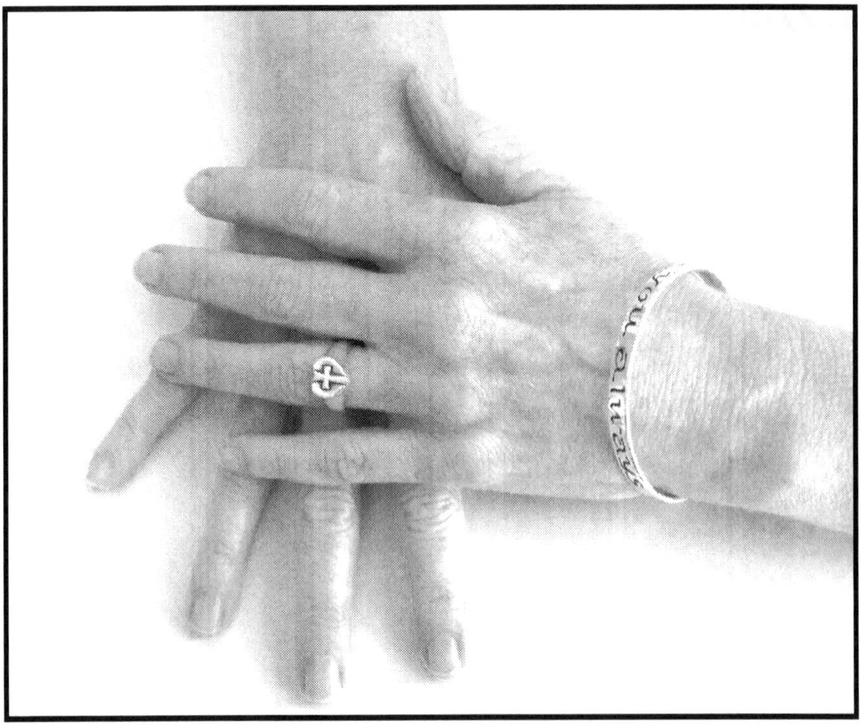

The real world (is) the world beyond plastic credit cards and traffic jams and word processors. –Madeleine L'Engle

Preface

This is a book about the real world. It is my story; the story of an ordinary life permeated with the sacred.

I've written this book for my children: two daughters, Shauna and Natalie, and two sons, Marcus and Preston, who, by the way, can complete my sentences. Like most mothers, I have a collection of expressions, some original and some borrowed. "Look beneath the lid," is one of my favorite originals. As a result of my tendency to *repeat* myself (ahem), my children can recite these *isms* in their sleep. You may not understand every term or inside joke on these pages, but you will get the gist of things for the most part.

By the time a woman reaches the last third of her life, she has accumulated a lot of stories. I have shared many of these with my husband, Vincent, who would often comment on how some of them were remarkable.

One day he said, "Becky, you have a lot of stories. You should write them down."

Several years passed before I responded to his nudges and started this project. I am grateful to him for his insistence even though it bordered on being the teensiest bit annoying at times. Thank you, Vincenzo.

What will you find in these pages? Thank you for asking. I think of this as a memoir, but it's really more of a collection. It is not a *sustained* narrative because, well, I cannot *write* a sustained narrative. You see, I am much more a speaker than a writer.

This collection includes *short* narratives, letters, conversations, a lot of journal entries, some (bad) poetry, meditations, and an appendix with a few spoken messages. One distinct advantage of this kind of reading is that you can breeze through a few pages at a time and easily put me back on the shelf.

Some of these lines were carefully written; others are clumsy and raw. They are all true. Nevertheless, I ask your forgiveness in advance if memory has failed me and details have been recorded inaccurately. The journal entries have been minimally altered only for the sake of clarity.

There are those parts of a family's history that are seen: where we were born, what place we call home, and so on. This collection is about the seen in part, but it is primarily a record of the *unseen* stories. A glimpse of the "real" world, as Madeleine L'Engle would say. These are stories of love, loss, forgiveness, healing, and redemption.

At rock bottom, this is the story of God walking with us through the joyful, the gut-wrenching and the ordinary.

The next few paragraphs are for Shauna, Natalie, Marcus, and Preston. If you have read this far and are not one of them, please stop now and turn to the first chapter. *Just kidding!*

This is your mother's story; therefore, it is a part of your history. As you will discover, however, it is incomplete. Some stories are not meant to be written. They are too intimate or too painful. You and I know what those stories are, and they will be remembered by us, "pondered in our hearts." Some of them are *yours* to tell and will remain so. Together we have walked through life, death, burial, and resurrection many times over.

Other stories are meant to be told, and they bear repeating. Here, I will repeat *again* what I hope is branded on your hearts and minds:

No mother could ask for more love from her children. Your affection, respect, and honor make me the richest lady in town. I marvel over how great the variation is among the four of you: vastly different personalities, gifts, philosophies, and perspectives. *Yet,* you love one another unconditionally and fiercely. Your commitment to each other is one of the greatest joys of my life.

I love our spirited discussions, which are made all the more fascinating because there are times when no two of us agree. What could be more fun? I am grateful that you read and think critically. I thank God that you *care* for others; your sensitivity runs deep. I watch you use your gifts and talents, doing what you *love* whether it "pays" or not, and that has made *you* the richest people in your respective towns.

I cherish the rare time alone I have with each of you, whether we are in the forest, on the beach, sitting on the porch swing, or talking over a good cup in a coffee bar. At that moment, I think, "Nothing could be more joyful than this!" And then the next time I am with a different one of you, I think the same thing: "Nothing could be more joyful than this!" Over and over it happens.

You are a gift, but you are not mine. I believe a mother raises her children to leave her, and you are a gift to the world and to your Creator.

Children of my body and heart, *remember* these stories. I love you.

Flagstaff, Arizona
February 2014

...the story of any one of us is in some measure the story of us all. For the reader, I suppose, it is like looking through someone else's photograph album. What holds you, if nothing else, is the possibility that somewhere among all those shots of people you never knew and places you never saw, you may come across something or someone you recognize. ...there is always the possibility that as the pages flip by, on one of them you may even catch a glimpse of yourself (and) the sacredness of your own journey.
Frederick Buechner

Brad and Becky, 1955

First Awareness

"How do you know if you're being mean to someone?" I asked my mother.

"God makes you feel sorry for them," she answered.

We were standing in the kitchen of our home when I asked. It was the simple question of a four-year-old child, and my mother's answer satisfied my curiosity. Who knows what prompted my question, but I tucked Mom's answer away in the folds of my mind.

Within a year, our family had moved from Nebraska, and we were living temporarily in Miami, Florida, where my father had a government contract for aerial spraying. It was the 1950s, after all, and humans had waged war on pests using large aircraft and strong chemicals. My brother and I were three and five years old, and we had no idea what was going on over our heads in the bright, sunny skies.

We stayed in an apartment complex in sunny Miami, and I remember a swimming pool.

Brad and I loved to squeal over and over, "It's MI-ami! No, it's MI-ami!"

An elderly woman named Hanlin had come with us from Nebraska, and she took care of Brad and me. She was timid and thin, and we thought she was ancient.

One day our parents were away, and we were under her care. We were especially ornery that day, and I remember her chasing us around the living room. Tow-headed Brad and I literally ran circles around the poor old woman, leaping across the sofa, around and around. I remember my delight in her not being able to catch us.

Suddenly, I stopped in my tracks. Out of nowhere, I remembered my mother's words from months earlier, and I realized *I felt sorry for Hanlin.*

I reasoned, "God just made me feel sorry for her because we are being mean."

It was the first time I remember consciously sensing God's presence. I corralled three-year-old Brad, and we stopped the running.

Joy on a Swing Set

Joy's trick is to supply
Dry lips with what can cool and slake,
Leaving them dumbstruck also with an ache
Nothing can satisfy.

Richard Wilbur
"Hamlen Brook"

My friend and I had already been to school and back home that day, but we liked to have the playground to ourselves. So after changing into play clothes and eating our after-school snacks, we two gangly eight-year-olds walked the block from our houses back to the playground at Kaibab Elementary School.

It was a dirt and concrete playground, which was typical of the desert schools in Phoenix. We played on the various pieces of equipment and eventually made our way to the swing set. It was a typical swing set with sturdy rubber seats and long, heavy chains that made our hands smell like metal. We could really get going on those swings, and higher and higher we went.

I was soaring through the air, and I leaned back while the breeze caught my hair and sent it in all directions. As always, it was great fun, but then something unexpected happened.

For no reason, my heart suddenly took wing. It was exhilarating, and a joy took hold of me that was so intense I thought I would burst! I had never experienced such rapture. I had never felt "so happy" and I even said something to my friend. It was a moment I would not forget.

The feeling departed as quickly as it had arrived, and I was back on earth again. My friend and I walked down the sidewalks and past the orange groves to our homes. We said goodbye, and I rushed into the house to tell my mother what had happened on the swing set.

Many years later, I learned that I was not alone in my experience. C. S. Lewis had also been "surprised by joy."

That experience on the swing set told me, "There is more."

The Farm

Glimpses of Childhood

My parents were social, loved practical jokes, and had a passion for adventure. Brad was funny and full of mischief, and I was the quieter one of the family. Mom made the best southern fried chicken and cream gravy in the world, and she iced her German chocolate cakes with thick, gooey coconut frosting. Silly Blackie, our dog, was also part of the family. Brad and I spent countless hours riding in the backseat of Dad's private aircraft or the family car. We traveled all the time, but it never occurred to us that this was out of the ordinary. We thought everyone traipsed around the continent.

During the school year, I spent many quiet afternoons playing in my bedroom. My imaginary world was usually composed of my very own classroom with me as the teacher. Even then, I loved solitude and quiet.

On top of the 1950s vintage hi-fi in our living room sat the family Bible, and its pages were always opened to a beautiful calligraphy of the Ten Commandments. As a child, I pored over those Commandments. I memorized them at a young age and naively determined that I would never break them. Reading those Commandments day in and day out made an indelible impression and is, perhaps, one reason I became a moral conservative long before I came to faith.

Brad and I spent joyful summers in two small towns and the farm country of southeastern Nebraska with cousins from both sides of the family. At the time, Shickley and McCool Junctions had approximate populations of 250 each. The long, carefree summer days were spent swimming with cousins in the town swimming pool or in my grandparents' large concrete horse trough situated in the middle of the farmyard. The girl cousins and I spent hours in the playhouse fighting off our spying boy cousins and making mud cookies.

Cousin LaMoine, who was four years older, would invent culinary nightmares made of mud, bugs and grass in her own playhouse and force me to eat them. She tormented Brad and me endlessly, which was the beginning of a lifelong relationship I count as one of the most cherished in my life. And, of course, beloved Aunt Theo was always in the wings loving and defending we little ones.

Two of the most cherished memories of my childhood took place at Grandma and Grandpa Biegert's farm near Shickley.

As a child from the Arizona desert, I spent many hours lying on my back in their yard, watching the wind toss the limbs of the towering old trees. To most children from North America, this would seem like nothing unusual, but for a child from the Arizona desert, this was out of the ordinary, and I never tired of it. I loved the Nebraska skies and how you could hear nothing besides the wind on those days. I loved the sky that seemed to go on forever, the solitude, and the cool grass beneath my young back. But most of all, I loved to watch the dancing trees that soared overhead.

The second memory can be summed up in three words: Grandma's brown bread. My grandmother was a farmer's wife, and her cooking is legendary. She made everything from scratch and never used a recipe. The bounty that was served on her round kitchen table was the result of fresh milk and cream, garden vegetables, eggs and chickens from the yard and cattle on the other side of the fence.

There was one item that was the family's favorite and that was Grandma's whole wheat bread. Still warm from the oven and slathered with creamy butter, we would gobble it up. Her bread was dark, sweet, and moist, and it was almost like eating cake. Grandma's brown bread was the ultimate comfort food and the stuff that dreams are made of!

As Brad and I entered adolescence, the summers in Nebraska changed. We would beg Grandma and Grandpa to let us drive on the gravel roads, which were as straight as arrows and lined with cornfields. Being a city kid, I was exhilarated to be allowed behind the wheel at the tender age of thirteen. One summer, LaMoine tried to teach me to shift a standard transmission, but it didn't take. Brad worked in the fields with our uncles and cousins, and I filled my time with dances and dates.

Summer after summer was spent in Nebraska, and we thought it would never end. But before I knew it, I was a young college student.

Surrender

I fled Him, down the nights and down the days;
I fled Him, down the arches of the years;
I fled Him, down the labyrinthine ways
Of my own mind; and in the mist of tears
I hid from Him, and under running laughter.

Francis Thompson
"The Hound of Heaven"

During my sophomore year of college, my family moved to Houston for a business opportunity. I got a summer job at a law firm in downtown Houston, and it was the hottest summer of my life. It was a steamy seven-block walk from the parking lot to the office, and by the time I arrived, I would be drenched— hair and makeup destroyed. Nevertheless, it was the beginning of Life. Tiny seeds were being planted.

The secretarial pool in which I worked would assign us to different desks where we would replace legal secretaries who were away on vacation. Midway through the summer, I was at the desk of a woman who was away, and the attorney for whom I worked seemed to be gone much of the time also. As a result, I had a lot of idle time.

During one particularly long day, I found some tracts by Norman Vincent Peale in the desk. Being bored out of my mind, I started reading them, and I discovered that I liked what I read. Because these were the days before the Internet, I jotted down the address of Peale's organization and sent a snail mail letter asking for more tracts. Soon thereafter, they were being mailed to our family's home in Houston.

A few months later, I was on my way to the University of Texas for the fall semester where I would be a junior transfer student, having decided that a small private university was not a good fit. Several friends and I were making the move together, and we were excited to be entering the world of a large state university. When I unpacked my belongings in our new apartment in Austin, I tossed the Peale tracts into my top desk drawer.

During the next month, I discovered that a university of 45,000 students was more than a little overwhelming. I felt lost and lonely, and I was living in "quiet desperation."

Up to this point, I had tried every legitimate thing I could think of to fill the void: education at a small, private college, even a sorority for a short time, friends, and now a state university. But the void remained. As I surveyed my emotional landscape, I thought, "If only I had a boyfriend, then I would be happy."

Sure enough, a boyfriend came along shortly thereafter. He and I were dating up a storm, seeing one another several times a week. It was not long, however, before it was apparent that we were not using the same moral compass. I knew I might lose the relationship, but I said no. He stopped calling.

This was the relatively minor straw that became more than I could bear on my own and that would open the door to the greatest turning point of my life. In the few days after he stopped calling, I was in despair. I had pursued happiness, but it was not about to be captured. I had failed.

A few nights later, I was alone in our college apartment and feeling miserably depressed. In contrast, my roommates had left for the evening and were out having a great time. It was October 2, 1971, a few days after my twentieth birthday. I was asking myself what had gone wrong and was probably analyzing my predicament from every possible perspective.

Then I remembered the tracts that I had received during the summer and which were now in my desk. I jumped out of bed, turned on the light, and picked up one. I read it like a starving woman would gobble up bread. It was about surrendering your life *to God*.

I remember thinking, "I have tried everything else, but I haven't tried God! Maybe that will 'make me happy.'" Yes, it was an entirely utilitarian approach to a relationship with God but one that He, in His mercy, would not reject.

I walked out of my bedroom, through the living room and onto the little deck that overlooked a dark city. I still remember how the stars looked as I stood in the darkness.

With my hands outstretched, I said, "God, I have tried everything, and I am so unhappy. I surrender my life to you." I did it just like the tract instructed, and I physically "threw" my life up to Him from my opened hands.

Words fail as I try to describe what happened next. The moment I threw my life up into the dark sky and gave it to God, a joy, a presence, and a power *blew* into my mind and body. Something *happened*. I was so shocked that I blurted out, "There really is a God!"

In my pajamas, I stood on the deck for a long time, drinking in this joy, awestruck and amazed. Something had happened, and I was changed.

Eventually, I made my way back to my bedroom. The apartment was quiet, and I crawled back into bed and turned off the light. It took a long time to fall asleep that night.

I had met the living God and would never be the same.

Becky, 1971

First Steps

But suddenly I heard the words of Christ and understood them, and life and death ceased to seem evil, and instead of despair I experienced happiness and the joy of life undisturbed by death.

Leo Tolstoy

After that night everything changed, and many small mercies followed. I remember a few and have probably forgotten many more.

The very next morning, I woke, dressed in my bell-bottom jeans, and began the walk to class as I always had. I made long strides toward campus, crossing Guadalupe Street, also called the Drag, which was the scene of many 1960s anti-war demonstrations. As always, Hare Krishnas in their bright orange tunics chanted and begged along the sidewalk.

As I walked the familiar route, I had a strong sense that this morning the walk was different. *I was not walking alone.* Whereas my heart had been desperate the evening before, now it was light and joyful. What a glorious morning it was! Nothing had changed, and everything had changed. *Someone walked with me.*

A few weeks later, I drove to Houston to spend the weekend with my parents. I could hardly wait to tell them about my new faith. As my parents listened with misty eyes, I remember a few of the things I said.

I explained as best as I could that I felt as if I had been *born again* even though I was "alive" before. I told them that *everything seemed new*, myself included. It was as if the trees were greener and the sky a brighter blue.

Little did I know that the Bible speaks of these very things. It would be some time before I discovered these verses:

No one can see the kingdom of God unless they are **born again**. John 3:3 [emphasis added]

Therefore, if anyone is in Christ **the new creation** *has come: The old has gone, the new is here!* II Corinthians 5:17 [emphasis added]

Slowly, I began to tell my closest friends what had happened to me on that night. One of my roommates responded, "Then you're a Christian, right?" I didn't know how to answer that question.

I stumbled and said, "Well, I guess I'm a Christian of sorts, but my experience was with God, not Jesus."

She looked totally confused, and I probably did, too. I did not know how Jesus fit into all of this. Years later, I would realize that I was a theist at that point, though I had never heard the term.

The following semester, I enrolled in a religion class and began to read the Bible. As I read the verses above, I remember thinking, "That's what happened to me! That is what I have experienced!" I could hardly believe that the New Testament language was so similar to my own. There was no mistaking that my experience was that of Christians in the early church. I recognized the handprints and realized that it was Jesus whom I had met that night while I stood on the deck in my pajamas.

As I ponder those early days as a believer, I think that one of the blessings of beginning at ground zero is that I arrived at faith's door with no preconceptions. Because I *experienced* it before I ever read about it in the Bible, I knew it was authentic, neither contrived nor imitated.

This One who was walking to class with me in a new way would be with me through all the years to come. And oh, how I would need Him. The very next year would bring one of the greatest losses of my life.

A Christmas Poem

Brad and I lived in different cities during my college years, but he was never out of my thoughts for long. He loved to tease and would start our telephone conversations with his deadpan, "Hello, idiot." My eyes would light up when I heard his voice. My love for Brad was fierce and protective, and I always knew his was for me. In spite of the love we shared, Brad struggled, and my heart ached.

A few months after my life-changing encounter with God, I remember lying on the floor in my college apartment. Music was blasting from the stereo. It was about this time that I had discovered the group James Gang and it inspired me to write a poem for Brad, probably because he liked heavy music, and it reminded me of him. It may have been "Funk 49" that fed my creative juices that night!

Lying on the shag carpeting, I penned the following words for Brad. After I had finished writing, I remember thinking how easily they had flowed, and I wondered if God had given the words to me.

Lest you think I have not noticed, I *know* this is a terrible piece of poetry, if it can even be called that. Its purpose was to communicate to Brad how very much I loved him, and it accomplished that. Later, I decided to decoupage it onto a small piece of wood, and I gave it to him on Christmas morning. How grateful I am, all these years later, that I expressed my love to him at this particular time.

It was to be Brad's last Christmas with us.

For Brad

Looking at you today makes it hard to believe
That you and I have grown together to be what we are
To think where we started and see where we've gone
Makes it seem so very long.

From "No, it's *MI*-ami!" to cartoons on Saturday mornings.
The time you ate the mud cookie from our playhouse.
And, of course, doing dishes—never without a fight.
Faking Rex off the haystack—a family laugh.
And our terrorizing ride in your loud car—Talk about fright!

You've put up with messy bathrooms
And listened to my love affairs.
I've never really said thanks
Or shown you how I care.

In your own way, you've loved me
Without even knowing
You were teaching *me* to love
And help me in my growing.

Thinking now, I can sincerely say
You're not an ordinary brother—not in any way.
No price could take you away.
Not in our *past* memories together or today.

Not much more can I say
That can help me convey...what we've shared together.
What you mean to me is something rare
I can best express in my simple prayer.

"Thank you, God, for giving me Brad.
Just to be with him makes me glad."

I love you,
Becky

Houston, Texas
December 25, 1971

The End of a Short Life

...in the midst of suffering there is a God who is with us and for us and will never let us go.

Frederick Buechner

It was the summer of 1972. Brad was eighteen years old and in trouble. His drug usage was taking its toll, and he was thin and defeated.

Mom, Dad, and I took a road trip from Houston to the beautiful Rockies of Colorado. Earlier in the summer, Brad had begun a road trip of his own, and it was arranged that he would meet us in Colorado. It was the last time we would all be together for more than a day or two.

When Brad arrived in Colorado, I was shocked at his appearance. He was terribly thin, and the ever-present ache that my heart carried for him grew sharper. His extensive road trip was planned so he could visit friends and relatives, and his next leg would be to Nebraska. Over the few days we were together, he asked me more than once to go with him, but I had a job waiting for me in Houston and could not join him. That I had to return to Houston was significant and part of *the plan*. Brad needed to go to Nebraska alone.

We parted ways for the time being, and Brad was on his way. What happened to Brad in the weeks that followed has always been unclear, but this is what I know.

After he arrived in Nebraska, Uncle John Biegert realized he was in trouble with his drug usage and wanted to help. He told Brad he would make a deal with him and that he had to see a pastor in Lincoln. John made the arrangements, and Brad went to see this man. Something extraordinary happened in that meeting, but I do not know what it was or how it happened.

What I do know is that in the short time that followed, Uncle John evidently witnessed an enormous change in Brad, and he wanted to celebrate. He held a special dinner in his home and invited family members, including relatives from the other side of the family tree. The purpose of the celebration was to honor Brad, and I remember being told that they made toasts to him and that Johnny made an especially funny and heartfelt speech. It must have been a beautiful evening. I can just imagine Brad's dimples as he tried to suppress that impish smile. He had turned a corner. Later, I would think of that evening as Brad's "last supper."

Shortly thereafter, Uncle John returned to Houston with Brad. By the time they arrived, only two weeks had passed since we had parted in Colorado, but I could hardly believe my eyes. Brad had gained about twenty pounds, and he looked better than he had in years.

Brad had made the decision to go to college that coming fall. We were all surprised and pleased as it had been a long time since he had been enthusiastic about anything. It was decided that I would go along with him to Southwest Texas State University since I "knew the ropes" and could help him register.

On the morning of our ride to San Marcos, Brad came downstairs to breakfast as I sat at the kitchen table. It was to be the last time we would share a meal and one that I have never forgotten for several reasons.

Mom was fixing something for us to eat, and we were chatting casually. Mom said something funny, and Brad *laughed hard*, a belly laugh. It was the first time I had heard Brad laugh in a long time. What followed was even more astounding.

Not casually, he said, "From now on, every day is going to be a holiday for me." You could have picked me up off the floor.

Mom, understandably wanting to add a touch of realistic thinking, said something like, "Well, not *every* day is a holiday."

Brad disagreed and said, "No, *every* day is going to be a holiday."

Less than twenty-four hours later, Brad would be absent from his body and from our lives.

Brad and I rode in his car from Houston to San Marcos with him at the wheel. It was a bright, sunny day, and he had the radio on. The song *Guitar Man* played, and I sang along. To this day, it is the song that most reminds me of him. It was so fun to be together, and there was now a new hope for his future.

We visited the college registrar's office and began our return trip to Houston. A few minutes later, we were at an intersection beneath an overpass when a man in a pickup truck broadsided us on Brad's side of the car. I was knocked unconscious. When I came to, I was spitting glass out of my mouth, and there was blood everywhere. The car was off the road. I looked at Brad and he was leaned against his door, unconscious. Mercifully, I could not see the injuries on the other side of his head, and in that moment I could not figure out where the blood had come from. He simply looked like he had fallen asleep. I laid my hand on him and said, "Brad, I'm right here, and I won't leave you." The engine was still running, so I reached over and turned the key off just as people came running to help.

An ambulance took us to a small regional hospital from which we were airlifted to a San Antonio hospital. We were both admitted, me for a minor concussion and glass cuts, and Brad for massive head injuries.

Our beloved Brad died in the night, on our father's birthday.

In the months that followed, everyone who knew our family recognized that something extraordinary had happened during Brad's final days on earth. In a matter of weeks, his life had gone from desperation to some sort of healing followed by a celebratory dinner given in his honor. And at breakfast on the day that he died, he had said, "From now on, every day is going to be a holiday for me." As we ate our breakfast that morning, we never dreamed what significance his words held.

He was dearly loved.

Max Bradley Biegert
February 16, 1954–July 26, 1972

Becky and Brad
1968

Grief: The Vacuum We Inhabit

The pupil dilates in darkness and in the end finds light, just as the soul dilates in misfortune and in the end finds God.

Victor Hugo

It was two weeks after Brad's death, and my head was still throbbing from the minor concussion I had sustained during our car accident. One night as I was preparing to go to bed, I was grumbling to myself about the pain.

During the night, I had a dream, and in it I relived the accident that took Brad's life. I felt the dull thud when the truck hit our vehicle, I felt my body jerk, and I heard the odd quiet of nothing other than the car engine when I "came to" in the passenger seat.

I awoke shaken, but I also *knew* something I had not realized before the dream. That is, that God had allowed my concussion so I would not *see* what happened to Brad. After that night, I did not complain about my headache any longer.

As my parents and I walked through the long grieving process, I was stunned when I realized that the heartache I had carried for Brad for so many years was *gone*. In its place was the sharp pang of loss and tears that I stifled far too often. One had replaced the other, but I no longer had to worry about Brad. He was safe now.

**Becky and Kids
1984**

**Shauna, Natalie, Marcus and Preston
1987**

Family Life

Dac...doo. Dacdoo!
Mah baby...
Bidda booda
La La, no!

August 1973 was a busy and stress-filled month. It had been a little over a year since Brad had died. I studied for my final exams, graduated from the University of Texas, prepared for a move to Dallas, and two weeks later I was married in Houston. It is no wonder that I was sick on my wedding day.

On the morning of our wedding, my father walked into my bedroom to wake me.

He said, "Becky, wake up. You are getting married today."

I looked up, leaned over the edge of the bed, and vomited. The day proceeded with great drama.

I started my period. Some sort of intestinal bug swept through the family, and we were dropping like flies. It was no respecter of persons; young and old alike were stricken. Relatives were throwing up in potted planters in the church foyer, and I limped down the aisle on my father's arm. Cousin LaMoine, a bridesmaid, had to sit down halfway through the ceremony. It was quite the memorable start to married life.

There were many moves in the next two decades from apartment to apartment, and even between cities. I loved moving and experiencing new places. There was Dallas, Philadelphia, Atlanta, Sedona, and finally Flagstaff.

These were the years of beginnings: establishing careers, starting a family, finding a church home, and creating traditions. Even though I loved to study and learn, there was nothing I wanted more during this season of my life than to be a stay-at-home mother. That, however, was not a given in those years.

In the 1970s, many women were juggling motherhood and careers while I believed passionately in the importance of raising my own children. Mine was not a popular position given the climate surrounding the "women's liberation" movement, but being out of sync with my generation was nothing new. In fact, I found it energizing to live counter-culturally.

Thankfully, graduate school for the children's father meant that his salary would enable me to stay home with our children. It had taken a cross-country move to Philadelphia, enrollment in an expensive two-year graduate program for him, and a move back to Dallas, but we had come full circle. Money was tight, but it was a tremendous relief and joy to be at home full time. I *loved* being a mother.

After the children's father completed his studies, we purchased our first house in the Lake Highlands area of Dallas. Shauna was ten months old at the time, and I remember a momentous morning at our new home.

It was the first day of his new job, and Shauna's father had left the house to drive to his office in downtown Dallas. I stood at the sink washing the breakfast dishes and looked out the small kitchen window. My thought was, "This is what I have always wanted. Millions of other homemakers are washing the breakfast dishes, and I am one of them. My dream has come true." It may sound silly, especially in light of cultural changes in the years since, but to me it was epic. I looked at motherhood as a noble calling, and I dove in.

*Many people have eaten my cooking and
have gone on to lead normal lives.*

Our family grew rapidly with four children being born within seven years. They were noisy, hectic years with the accompanying exhaustion, but I cherished them. The beauty of a young family was captured late one night as we were driving home after visiting relatives in Mississippi. The children's father was driving, and I sat in the middle row of our large SUV with Marcus and Preston. Shauna and Natalie were in the "way back" singing. Preston was nursing, and Marcus leaned his head against me. I thought, "It doesn't get any sweeter than this."

In the midst of diapers and games and lots of little kisses, I continued to read to quench my intellectual thirst. Sometimes it would only be a few pages in bed before I would fall asleep. As the children grew, I took night classes at a local seminary and participated in study groups. It was a full and rich season.

As we outgrew houses, there were more moves within Dallas. When Preston was one, we moved to our house on Club Glen where I thought we would live for the rest of our lives. It had a large yard with a great tree house and plenty of room for friends.

During those years, we had a "second home" which was our church. We had wonderful friends, great teachers (many of whom were seminary professors), and activities for everyone. Friendships were formed and they have endured through the years and across the miles.

Our lives changed tremendously when we moved to Arizona in 1989. We went from a large, conservative southern city to a forest home outside a small, liberal mountain town in the west. Everyone in the family took downhill ski lessons, and during ski season we spent most weekends on the slopes. There were literally thousands of acres at our doorstep for hiking, exploring, and riding ATVs. These were the years of school programs, team sports, church youth group activities, and joyful Christmas parties that filled the house with families and carols.

But all was not well.

Rupture

On April 24, 1997, my husband of twenty-four years and the father of our four children left the family. You never think it will happen to you.

It is the greatest sorrow of my life that my children have experienced the brokenness of their parents' divorce. The following pages contain journal entries that tell part of that sad story.

The Hardest of the Hard Years

April 24, 1997

On this day, he moved out and left our family. Unbelievably and as God would have it, this was my Scripture reading for the day:

Those who sow in tears will reap with songs of joy. He who goes out weeping, carrying seed to sow, will return with songs of joy, carrying sheaves with him.

Psalm 125:5-6

Early in the day, he and I called Shauna in Waco, Texas, where she was attending college. We called so he could tell her that he was leaving. She cried, of course. After the younger three children came home from school, he told them the same. We sat in the living room, and they listened in stunned silence while he spoke the words. He rose, said his goodbyes and walked out the front door.

Later in the day and after he had left, Shauna called me back. God love her. She said, "Mom, how are you doing?"

I said, "Well, honey, I'm not doing so well."

She asked, "How so?"

I said, "Well, I can't sleep, and let's just say I'm spending a lot of time in the bathroom."

"I didn't need to know that," she responded.

I continued, "I've lost thirteen pounds in two weeks."

Incredulous, she asked, "You've lost thirteen pounds?" She paused. "Maybe *I* can lose thirteen pounds!"

And I laughed. I never dreamed I would be able to laugh on what was the saddest day of my life.

April 25, 1997

"Mom, what will we do for groceries?"

May, 1997

"I think God has forgotten all about us, Mom."

May 3, 1997

These verses sustain me and give me hope:

I waited patiently for the Lord, and He inclined to me, and heard my cry. He brought me up out of the pit of destruction, out of the miry clay; and He set my feet upon a rock, making my footsteps firm. And He put a new song in my mouth, a song of praise to our God, Many will see and fear, and will trust in the Lord. Psalm 40:1-4

Father, I don't know how you are going to answer, but I know you have heard my cry and will send help. Thank you, Father.

My soul waits in silence for God only, from Him is my salvation, He only is my rock and my salvation, my stronghold. I shall not be greatly shaken. My soul, wait in silence for God only. For my hope is from Him. He only is my rock and my salvation, my stronghold, I shall not be shaken. On God my salvation and my glory rest. The rock of my strength, my refuge is in God. Trust in Him at all times, O people; pour out your heart before Him. God is a refuge for us! Psalm 62:1-8

Though the fig tree should not blossom, and there be no fruit on the vines, though the yield of the olive should fail, and the fields produce no food, though the flock should be cut off from the fold, and there be no cattle in the stalls, yet I will exult in the Lord, I will rejoice in the God of my salvation! The Lord God is my strength; and he has made my feet like hind's feet and makes me walk on my high places. Habakkuk 3:17-29

May 13, 1997
For the third time in less than a week, I have read or heard a devotional on Esther. What am I to learn from her? She was strong-willed, determined and used her position for good, for God's glory and not personal gain. She was born "for such a time as this." Was I born for such a time as I am in now—to glorify God? Help me do that, Father.

September 6, 1997
Today Princess Diana was buried. The boys and I spent the day with Mom. On the way home, I told them I never thought that I would be divorced or a single mom and that I was doing the best job I could. Marcus said, "Well, you're doing a very good job."

April 30, 1998
Today as I was driving, this thought came to mind. I don't know if I heard it somewhere or if it's original. The more I lose, the less there is on this earth to hold my affection. I look to things that will last forever. And to heaven.
Again today, Preston was cheering me up with funny jokes and music.

July 3, 1998
Tonight Natalie reminded me of how the month before her dad left (I knew he was preparing to leave, but the kids didn't know yet) she would come into my room night after night and share something out of her quiet time. And what she shared was you, Father, speaking to me. She had never done that before. What a wonderful reminder of your loving hand over us.
In the last year, Father, you have brought the verse from Esther to my mind over and over and over. For this purpose I was made.

Veil

In the weeks and months following the departure of the children's father, the stress, conflict, and heartache were nearly unbearable. My children's grief ripped my heart apart. We were subdued and uncharacteristically quiet. And their questions. O God, how does a mother answer the confusion of four teenagers whose family is in the process of being destroyed? Over and over, I begged God for wisdom and strength.

On one of those early days, I asked thirteen-year-old Preston how he was doing. He answered, "Just trying to make it." I think that describes how we all felt; we were just trying to survive.

My attempt to survive was not measured by taking it one day at a time. That would have been overwhelming. I only hoped to make it from hour to hour; it was that hard. The divorce process was staggeringly harsh and damaging. There were days and nights when I feared for my sanity, and the nights were especially hard as it seemed like the pain closed in after darkness fell.

We took mattresses from their rooms, and for weeks all the children slept scattered in my large bedroom until they could bear to return to their own rooms again. After we turned out the lights, I would pray a blessing aloud over our torn and bleeding family. There was comfort in being together during those early nights. And there would be small and large mercies all along the rocky path.

One mercy that still astounds me is what I refer to as the veil. A few months into what I refer to as the "hard years," I awoke one morning with a new sensation. At first, I thought something was wrong with my eyes. It was as if someone had pulled gauze or a veil over my eyes. I could *see* but everything looked gray. Even sound seemed muffled.

After this sensation persisted for several days, I went to the doctor. My eyes and ears were checked, appropriate questions were asked, and the physician found nothing wrong. I returned home and slowly became accustomed to the veil. At first it had been troubling and annoying, but it eventually became the new normal.

Another mercy during this time was the faithfulness of a dear friend who lived across the country. She was my only Christian friend who had experienced a divorce under similar circumstances. She and I would talk about once a month during this time, and she gave me hope. She had walked the same path, and I counted on her for counsel and prayer.

During one of our conversations, I told her about the veil. I described the phenomenon and told her I had no idea what it was.

She listened and responded, "I remember that."

"What?" I asked.

She repeated, "I remember that. The same thing happened to me. It lasted for months and eventually lifted."

I was relieved to know that I was not imagining it, and it was also comforting to know that it would end.

After a *year or two*, the veil lifted. I am not sure I remember the exact time; I just realized one day that it was gone. As I look back on it now, I see it as a gift from God. The veil softened the harshness and conflict that threatened to swallow me. It was like a cushion that absorbed some of the blows. Perhaps it was a stage of post-traumatic stress disorder. By the time the fog lifted, the shock had passed and with it much of the tearing and bleeding.

What a strange and welcome haze it had been.

An Unexpected Gift

In the late 1990s, I was learning to be a single mother, and part of that entailed taking care of the finances. Whereas I was initially intimidated, I learned that I was actually pretty good at it. I enjoyed keeping a neat set of books, setting money aside for savings, and working within a budget. I had seen God's faithfulness in every aspect of our lives since the divorce, and that included His financial provision. I made the decision to increase our giving to the Lord's work. It was a joy to give a bit more back to Him, and I told the children.

A few years earlier and as part of the divorce settlement, I had to assume significant debt in order for the children and me to stay in our house on Hidden Hollow. Each month I would write a check to the bank, and I groaned each time. It would take forever to be out of debt.

Then, one summer day, I sat at my desk paying bills and writing checks. As I wrote the hefty check to the bank once again, I groaned as usual. But then, something unexpected occurred. Out of nowhere, the words came from my lips, "Father, somehow please pay this debt off before the end of the year."

What? Where did that come from? I had no idea why I said that prayer, and it seemed a completely unreasonable request. I finished my desk work and went on with the day. Several months passed and I forgot my prayer.

One day in the late fall my father called and had news. He told me that my deceased uncle's estate had been settled and that I, along with my five cousins, would be receiving some money. This was a surprise to me because my uncle had died quite some time ago, and I had assumed that the estate was already settled. My father did not know how much money we cousins would receive. I waited.

It was now the Christmas season. Marcus, Preston and I were on our way to Christmas Eve services in Flagstaff, and I stopped at the mailboxes at the end of our dirt road, grabbed the mail from our box, and tossed it on the dashboard. We arrived at church early (a minor miracle), so I told the boys to go in and find seats. I would look through the mail and follow in a few minutes.

I still remember what a cold, dreary day it was, and I can still picture the gray skies as I sat in our warm car in the parking lot. As I leafed through the envelopes, I saw a return address from my uncle's attorney. Holding my breath, I opened the envelope. Inside was a letter and a substantial check. When I saw the amount, I whispered, "Oh my goodness. Oh my goodness. Oh my *goodness!*"

I remembered the prayer that had tumbled from my mouth during the summer and which was from Someone other than myself, the prayer that asked God to pay the debt before *the end of the year.* It was December 24.

When Marcus, Preston and I returned home from church that night, I told them all about it.

Marcus said, "I think God wants to see if we will still give Him more." Sure enough, we gave Him more as I had decided months earlier, *and* the debt was completely paid off. There was a small amount left over.

Yellow is for mail because mail is like sunshine.

CROOKED TREE

*The world is full of darkness, but...at the heart
of darkness whoever would
have believed it? – there is joy unimaginable.*

Frederick Buechner

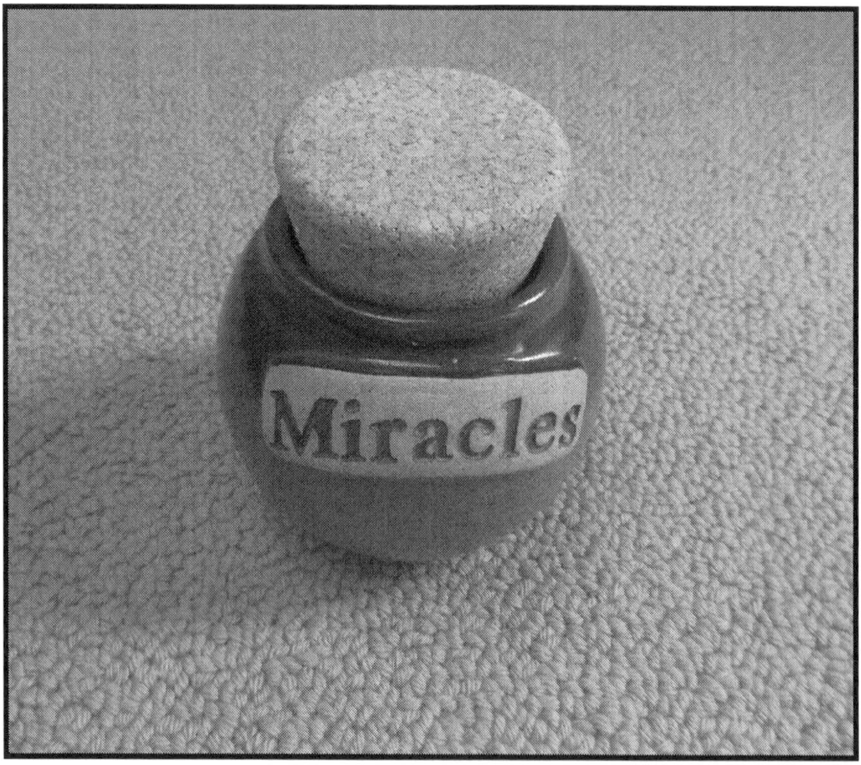
Miracles

Onto the Miracles Jar

Following the divorce in 1997, I made the decision that I would not date until all of my children had graduated from high school. They needed time to heal, and so did I.

There is a large blue pottery jug on my bathroom counter. It has a large cork lid, and the front is etched with the word, Miracles. For many years, it has been the visual reminder of what lies within.

Inside are a number of God-sized requests that I have scribbled on pieces of scratch paper. Each request is so grand and so huge that only God could bring it to pass. This is not a place for the faint of heart or for small, easily accomplished requests. It holds only outlandish requests that could qualify as miracles were they to come to pass.

So it was that in October of 2000, at the age of forty-nine, and two years before I would allow myself to date, I jotted down the following words and placed them in my Miracles jar:

A godly man who loves the Lord, me and my children. Fun-loving!

Father, according to your will and in your time.

Becky

Seminary: A Dream Realized

Years before, in the fall of 1973, I was newly married and living in Dallas. I wanted to study theology and applied to a local seminary. Lo and behold, I received a response that chastised me. This particular seminary did not believe women should be pastors, did not admit women to their programs, and encouraged me to go to a Bible study at my local church. I was incensed. Why was it frowned upon for a woman to study theology?

Over the next thirty years and as time allowed, I read voraciously, studied theology informally, and took extension classes to feed my hunger. I could not get enough, and my dream of attending seminary never faded.

In my greatest imagination, I could not have foreseen the incredible gift that awaited me.

After Preston, my youngest child, graduated from high school in 2001, it was time for me to transition from a full-time, hands-on mother to...what? It took me about three minutes to decide. It was time to study theology formally and in residence.

Journal entries follow.

October 1, 2001, Vancouver, BC

Today Preston and I visited Regent College. It is in one building on the campus of the University of British Columbia, by the water in a beautiful suburb. It's so pretty. My interview was great. The admissions guy told me that TODAY was the deadline for winter applications. Today! I had no idea. I submitted my application on the spot. He looked at my transcripts and said I would have no problem getting into the program.

I like the school. It's small and in such a pretty area. The program looks good—tough academically. I would love to come here to this beautiful city for two years. Father, it sounds so heavenly. Please bring it to pass.

Saturday, December 1, 2001, Vancouver, BC

Met Natalie at airport in Vancouver, got the rental car and took off to hunt for my new apartment. Drove into an area called Hampton Place and up to the first building, which has a locked entrance. A girl happened to be walking into the building, and I spoke to her before she went in. I told her I was looking for an apartment, and she directed me to the manager who said a man was there at that moment with a place to rent. He showed us the apartment, and it's beautiful. It's the very first place we visited! The former renters had been there for three months while teaching at Regent and had just moved out. The owner was having the carpet cleaned. Father, what a gift! I am overwhelmed! The apartment is beautiful—two bedrooms and only one mile from Regent. I can walk to class!

Thursday, December 27, 2001, Leaving Flagstaff and on the way to seminary!

The adventure begins! Yesterday was long, but Shauna and I got everything in the car and got to bed at 2 a.m. Telling Marcus and Preston goodbye was hard. They were so sweet, said "I love you," kissed my cheek and gave me long hugs. Shauna and I cried when we left. Such a mixture of feelings—bittersweet.

Under Heaven

Dallas. Steel. Concrete and freeways. The roar of rush hour. Gray skies. Flat land and few trees. Southern cooking and southern hospitality. Black-eyed peas and cornbread. Friends, lots of friends. A loving church. Four little ones underfoot. *Children are a gift of the Lord.* An intact family. Distant thunder. An approaching storm? Dinner parties. Laughter. Family traditions. Practical jokes. Birthday parties in the backyard. Dallas.

Flagstaff. Gigantic ponderosa pines. Wildflowers. A cedar cabin in the forest with a view of the mountain. A porch swing. What we had always wanted. The wind in the trees. First snow. Brilliant stars. Teenagers. Youth group parties. Games in the forest. Prayer partners. Bright blue skies. Walking through the forest with the dogs. *This is the day which the Lord has made; let us rejoice and be glad!* Bonfires on fall evenings. Birkenstocks and blue jeans. Flagstaff!

The storm? I hear it again. It's close now. *Be anxious for nothing but make your requests known to God.* Secrets. Smiling on the outside, aching on the inside. Protect the children, protect the children.

Loud, angry thunder. *Fear not for I am with you.* Questions. And searching for answers. God, can't somebody tell us what is wrong? *Be still and know. I am God.*

Rain. Unrelenting beating against the windowpanes. Leaks in the ceiling. Cracks of lightning. A direct hit on the chimney, cracking it all the way to the foundation. Wind, whipping and blowing, slamming rain into the sides of the trembling house. O Jesus, it is all breaking apart. *My child, I will never leave you nor forsake you.*

Pain around every corner. Shock. Numbness. Exhaustion. *Come unto me all who are weary, and I will give you rest.* The destruction of a family. The children. O God, the children. *The Lord draws near to the brokenhearted.*

The final rupture. He is leaving. O Jesus, help us. *I am with you.* Phone calls. Tears. Prayer partners. More tears. The Holy Spirit: Comforter, Healer, the Balm of Gilead. *I waited patiently for the Lord; and He inclined to me, and heard my cry.*

My soul waits in silence for You only; From You is my salvation. You only are my rock and my salvation. My hope is from You.

There are windows to wash, holes to putty, and a chimney to patch. Pine needles in the yard need raking. Water stains on the furniture need attending, too. *Those who wait upon the Lord shall renew their strength.*

The clouds are lifting. We can see the mountain again. *I will lift up my eyes to the mountains—where does my help come from? My help comes from the Lord, the Maker of heaven and earth.* Quiet nights by the fire. The prayers of our brothers and sisters. Salve for our aching hearts.

Weeping endures for a night, but joy comes in the morning. Dawn is breaking. First light peeking through the trees, bathing the steaming forest. Sitting in my robe on the porch swing with a mug of hot coffee. The mountain.

He brought me out of the pit of destruction, out of the miry clay; He set my feet upon a rock making my footsteps firm. He put a new song in my mouth, a song of praise to our God; Many will see and fear, and will trust in the Lord.

There is an appointed time for everything. There is a time for every event under heaven—a time to weep, a time to laugh, a time to mourn, a time to dance.

Thank you, Father. It is time to dance!

Vancouver, British Columbia
April 2002

REBECCA BIEGERT CONTI

Porch Swing

Dating

January to July 2002 were some of the most intellectually stimulating, painful, *and* joyful months of my life. I moved from Flagstaff to Vancouver, British Columbia, to study theology, a lifelong dream. The city and seminary exceeded my expectations. However, I was living alone for the first time in my life and was far away from my family, some of who needed me. It was a season of sharp contrast between the bitter and the sweet.

During these months and for the first time in nearly thirty years, I began to date. I began a long-distance relationship with a kind, intelligent man in the United States who was part Italian and with whom I had much in common. As the relationship progressed, it became apparent that he and I were not on the same spiritual page, but I did not trust my judgment. After having waited five years since my divorce to begin dating again, I vacillated and was reluctant to end the relationship. *Yes, I will. No, I can't. Yes, I must. No, I shouldn't.* I was paralyzed and afraid that I would make a mistake I would regret. I asked God to make it clear to me. And that He would do...at the bottom of the Grand Canyon, no less.

During the summer break from classes I returned to Flagstaff so I could spend time with family. Through the help of a friend, Natalie and I were able to secure reservations for a five-day guided white water rafting trip down the Colorado River in the Grand Canyon. What should have been the fun trip of a lifetime turned into something far different—and profound.

Journal entries follow.

Grand Canyon at 115 Degrees

Tuesday, July 30, 2002, Grand Canyon (descending into hell)

Hit the trail at 4:15 a.m. so we could beat the heat. Natalie and I were in the first group to go down. Still dark and needed a flashlight. Got the shakes from Gatorade. The clasp on my swimsuit top broke on the way down. Knees, especially the right one, killing me. Ended up using trekking poles as crutches. I was the very last one to the bottom, and everyone in our group had to wait for me. By the time I got to the river, it was 115 degrees. The big toenail on my right foot flipped off because my hiking boots are too tight. I can hardly move because of the pain in my knee. I'm paying money for this?

Started down the river on our raft, went through one set of great rapids and reached the campsite for the first of five nights. My bladder is shutting down, and I can't urinate. The heat blasting from the canyon walls is like a furnace; it's so hot I can hardly sleep. This must be what hell is like. I can see bats against the night sky. Got up in the night to try to urinate; the area was covered in scorpions.

Wednesday, July 31, 2002, Grand Canyon (by the water's edge)

Hit the river at 7:15 a.m. It is so HOT, but the water is too COLD for us to swim so we can't cool off. My knee is better, but the big toenail on my other foot has lifted off, too. I can't take any of the day hikes with the group because of my injuries. The verse, "God chastens those whom He loves," keeps running through my mind. I am in excruciating pain because my bladder is full, and I still can't urinate.

We stopped for a hike. Natalie offered to stay with me, but I insisted that she enjoy the hike. I stayed alone by the river after the group left. By this time, my bladder is distended. I am scared. I kneeled under a scrub tree near the edge of the river for some shade, and I pondered the situation: "I am trapped here, and there is no way out. I feel like Jonah sitting under the bush for shade after having run from God." Again, I tried to urinate. Nothing.

I whispered, "God, what do you want me to do?" I felt Him with me, here in hell. Then, I knew what this was about. I needed to end the relationship with the man I had been dating. After months of wondering, I finally had clarity. I knew this was of God, and I knew it was right. He had made Himself clear. I said, "Yes, I will Father. Thank you."

Within seconds and with God as my witness, urine flowed. There in the bottom of the Grand Canyon near the Colorado River, it flowed again and again and again until my aching bladder was empty.[1] It had been over twenty-four hours by this time.

My heart overflowed with gratitude and wonder.

My daughter, do not despise the Lord's discipline and do not resent his rebuke, because the Lord disciplines those he loves, as a father the daughter he delights in.

Prov. 3:11–12

---

[1] I am indebted to the leader of my Flagstaff writing group, Mary K. Johnson, for informing me that Martin Luther was spiritually enlightened during a struggle with constipation. It makes me a tad less embarrassed to know that I have such esteemed company in my somewhat similar affliction. (See *In the Beginning*, Dr. Alister McGrath, 2001, Doubleday)

Bath

Your word washes over me
like a warm bath,

soothing my dryness,
cleansing me,
lifting my spirit.

Vancouver, British Columbia
2002

Aching Loneliness

After the encounter at the bottom of the Grand Canyon, I made it out alive with a lot of bruises and missing toenails to show off. As soon as I returned to Hidden Hollow, I called the man I had been dating and gently told him the story of what had happened and that our relationship could not continue. It was both an ending and a beginning that I could not yet see.

A few weeks later, I left Flagstaff and returned to Vancouver to study for the fall semester. What follows is a partial record of events that occurred over the next few months.

September 10, 2002, Vancouver, BC

I am lonely, Father. Please provide for me.

January 11, 2003, Vancouver, BC

I am starting the New Year without a relationship. It will be interesting to see what the year brings. I need more friends who are my age.

A Strange Prayer

Mid-January 2003, Vancouver, BC

Father, please give me a husband. And make him Italian.

The night I said this prayer aloud, I had kneeled next to the bed in my apartment. The first sentence came from me. It was my heart's cry and an admission of the aching loneliness.

The second sentence, however, did not come from me. I was surprised as soon as I heard the words tumble from my lips because, for one thing, I was living in very fair, very *British* Columbia with nary an Italian in sight. In other words, it was an *unreasonable* thing to ask. Besides, what woman would ask the Lord for a husband and then specify his ethnicity?

"Where did *that* come from?" I thought. Very soon, I would discover why Someone had given me those exact words.

Praise Man

Toward the end of January 2003, I "met" a man online whose screen name was "Praise Man." I discovered that he was a worship leader, which explained the nickname. We started corresponding through the website, and his heart for God was evident. We wrote to one another about our families, ministry, and our relationship with God. He told me that he had been widowed, and we discussed theology. I began to look forward to his emails each day. After a week or so, he asked if I would like to bypass the website, give one another our real names, and email personally. I agreed.

He sent his address to me first, and I saw, "vincentconti@hotmail.com." I looked at his name and immediately recognized the last name as *Italian*.

I blinked, smiled and blurted out, "God, what are you up to?"

Awkward Phone Call
Aka
Daughter Freaks Out

February 2003, Vancouver, BC

Becky: "I have met a wonderful, godly man online."

Shauna: "You met a man *online*?"

Becky: "Yes, on a Christian website. We just exchanged email addresses. His name is Vincent."

Shauna: "You told him your real name??"

Becky: "Yes, Shauna. It's safe and besides, he lives in Connecticut."

Shauna: "You *think* he lives in Connecticut! He could be a serial killer!"

Timing Is Everything

Sometimes we have to suffer before we can die.
Sometimes we have to suffer before we can live.

Vincent Conti

When I "met" Vincent online, we lived on opposite sides of North America, he in Connecticut while I was living in British Columbia. There were other obvious differences. He is an urban Yankee and the grandson of Italian immigrants. I am the offspring of Germans and Scots with roots in the Midwest and southern United States. I mean, we are talking about serious cultural differences here: Italian sausage or black-eyed peas? "Kaw-fee" or sweet tea?

When I was studying in Vancouver, most of my fellow students were in their twenties and thirties. As much as I valued and enjoyed those friendships, I was in my early fifties and had more in common with my professors. I longed for relationships with people closer to my own age. For that reason, I began cruising a Christian website. I enjoyed corresponding with peers who were interested in spiritual things.

In the meantime, Vincent was living in central Connecticut where he was recovering from a string of sorrows. He had cared for his dear wife during her battle with cancer. She died at the age of fifty, and some time later he suffered a heart attack.

While he was convalescing at home, time was heavy on his hands. As a result, he checked out a Christian website, something he would not have done under normal circumstances.

Timing is everything. The Lord brought us together in cyberspace, and I fell in love with his heart.

I will restore to you the years that the swarming locust has eaten. Joel 2:25

New Chapter

*Our hearts are like stone and only suffering carves them
into bowls big enough to catch the joy.*

Michael O'Brien

Over the next year, Vincent and I traveled between British Columbia, Connecticut, and Arizona numerous times. We were introduced to one another's families *and* to the differences between our lives—different Christian traditions, a northeastern urban lifestyle as opposed to life in a western forest, and even our accents!

Vincent traveled to Vancouver in September 2003 and asked me to marry him. We were looking out over Vancouver Bay on a day of sunshine and bright blue skies. We were sitting on a bright blue sofa, and his engagement ring was a blue sapphire, my birthstone. Everything was blue except for our hearts! Following Vincent's widowhood and my divorce, God was beginning a new chapter in our lives.

In the months that followed, we had many decisions to make and numerous logistical challenges. For one thing, I had not yet completed my studies at Regent College. Second loomed the question of where we would live. Connecticut? Arizona? Vancouver? It was decided that we would be married in January 2004, and that we each would make our respective moves to Flagstaff. I would complete my last few seminary courses by correspondence.

It would be wonderful to once again live closer to my family and to live in the beautiful ponderosa pine forest, but I was uncertain about living in the Hidden Hollow house. The walls held so much pain, and I did not know if I could bear the memories, even with Vincent at my side. He suggested we give it a year, and I agreed. Little did I know how difficult it would be.

Healing

Barely three months after we had married and moved back to Flagstaff, I awakened one morning with uncharacteristic tears. The memories felt like a lead apron on my chest. It seemed as if every room, every corner, and even the yard reminded me of unbearable pain. I told Vincent I did not know if we could stay and make it our home. What followed was one of the most healing experiences of my life.

Vincent said he wanted to walk through the house with me, and he wanted me to name each and every memory, room-to-room. We began. We walked through every room, even some closets, the hallway, the staircase, the bathrooms, the front porch, back deck, yard, garage, and driveway. In each spot, I spoke the painful memory. Then, he would pray over that place and that memory. He prayed using powerful metaphors and words that were not a part of my own Christian tradition. It took quite some time, and I know it was hard for him to hear all of the stories.

What happened? God lifted the pain surrounding Hidden Hollow from my memories and from my heart. It was *gone*.

With the healing, we could begin to re-create Hidden Hollow into what would eventually become Hidden Hollow Prayer Retreat, a place to rest and pray. It would be a place of refuge and rest for our families and for us. It would be a place where people could pray and spend time alone with God. It would be a place where God was glorified, as I had always hoped.

> *This is the resting place. Let the weary rest.*
> Isaiah 28:12

Hidden Hollow Prayer Retreat

Hidden Hollow Prayer Walk

Land of the Living

Tuesday, April 1, 2004, Flagstaff

My last few seminary courses are behind me, and I have completed the program. Father, you enabled and sustained me. Vincent and I now begin a more normal life.

He is upstairs practicing piano for the Good Friday and Easter services. It looks like rain—a welcome sight. My Scripture reading for today:

I am still confident of this: I will see the goodness of the Lord in the land of the living. Wait for the Lord; be strong and take heart and wait for the Lord.

Psalm 27:13–14

Yes, Father, I have waited, and I am seeing your goodness anew. I am in the land of the living.

A(nother) True Story

I have good news, and I have bad news.

Once upon a time, Offspring M, who enjoys exhilarating activities, wanted to engage in a decidedly high-risk activity, in an even higher-risk setting, which would exacerbate the already dangerous nature of the activity. Parent D invited Offspring M to join him in a series of classes that would teach them how to engage in the activity in a skilled manner. Parent D and Offspring M registered for the classes and were preparing for the series.

On February 19, 2005, Offspring M told Parent R about the classes. Because of Offspring M's age and particularly the setting in which he would engage in the activity, Parent R was terribly concerned. She began praying that God would give wisdom, protect, and even stop this from occurring although she did nothing to interfere. Neither did she speak to Parent D about the matter. The classes were set to begin on a Saturday morning, and Parent R was afraid and praying fervently.

On Monday morning, February 24, 2005, Parent R, having assumed that the classes had begun the previous weekend, answered the telephone's ring. Offspring S was calling Parent R and immediately asked the question, "Have you been praying that Offspring M wouldn't go to the class?"

Parent R answered, "Yes. Why?"

"Well," Offspring S explained, "On the night before the class, Parent D fell and injured himself seriously so neither he nor Offspring M will be able to take the class."

Parent R exclaimed, "What? Are you serious? Offspring S! I would never pray that harm come to Parent D!"

Offspring S responded, "Oh, I know *that*. But, I *knew* you had been praying!"

Scattered Loved Ones

Monday, October 11, 2004, Flagstaff
    Father, please provide a way for us to spend time with Vincent's family. Bring them here or us there. Somehow.

Tuesday, April 12, 2005, Flagstaff
    Back from Connecticut again. Vincent needs to be with his family more... Father, your will be done. Prepare the way for us to spend more time there.

Thursday, June 7, 2005, Flagstaff
    Vincent's dad has a kidney stone, and his mom is deteriorating. The top floor of Vincent's multi-family is going to be vacated. Father, if you will, open up a way (financially) for us to keep it for ourselves.

Sunday, December 4, 2005, New Britain, Connecticut
    I am having so much fun setting up housekeeping and decorating (our new little apartment)...Thank you so much, Father, for this gift.

Serving God Together

Monday, February 26, 2007, Flagstaff

What a weekend! We set up for the church's prayer retreat on Friday night. I went to bed unhappy with my introduction to Guided Contemplative Prayer, but I had done my best and committed it to God. At 4:30 a.m., I woke up with the intro in my mind. I jumped up and wrote it all down. I was so excited I could hardly go back to sleep. When I got up in the morning, I re-typed the intro.

(After all these years) I am still so in awe when God does something like this! It also reminded me that this matters and that He really wants to bless these people. Well, bless them He did! It was such a joy to watch them go through the stations and to meet God there. What a privilege!

Vincent's music blessed the people. He said when I gave the intro that people nodded, and he could see relieved looks on people's faces. It was exactly what they needed to hear as they tried something new to them and different from their church's tradition.

What Has Come to Pass

Friday, June 13, 2008, Flagstaff
I was taking a few old books to Bookmans to trade in. One was Growing Through Divorce. *Cheerful title. Not. When I read it years ago I jotted on the inside cover things I wanted to do. This is the list I found:*

- retreat center
- bed & breakfast
- teach speech at NAU
- master's degree in theology
- missions trips

All of these have come to pass except for teaching at NAU which was actually the least desired one.
And, wouldn't you know it? My Scripture reading for today:
Consider what God has done. Ecclesiastes 7:13

An Old Friend

Saturday, May 2, 2009, Flagstaff

We are back from Connecticut. The breeze in the ponderosa pines sounds like an old friend.

Uncle Barney and Black-eyed Peas

Tuesday, May 12, 2009, Flagstaff

Beloved Uncle Barney died Thursday morning. The time with family and at the memorial service was precious. It was a sweet southern service, and the little Bayou Scie Church in Zwolle (Louisiana) even furnishes fans for the ladies. The church ladies fixed a lunch afterward with the best of southern cooking, including pepper gravy, black-eyed peas, cornbread from heaven, sweet potatoes, collard greens, fresh green beans with bacon, and homemade peach cobbler.

When I started greeting relatives and looking around the room, I thought, "This is love."

When Our Pain Blesses Others

Monday, May 18, 2009, Flagstaff

Yesterday was a day to remember. I preached at our church, and the message was God's. I spoke on fear, and I told the story of Brad's life and death. As I spoke, I could tell the words were resonating with the people. Afterwards I invited them to come up for prayer. A woman walked forward and told me her sister had died three weeks earlier in a car accident and that her addicted daughter was in trouble.

I said, "This hit a little too close to home, didn't it?" She said the message was for her. Then, a young woman told me that the message was for her mother-in-law who was there on that day and was gripped by fear. Wow.

To Our Doorstep

Saturday, November 21, 2009, Flagstaff

On Thursday, I asked God to show me how to bless others in need, and yesterday you, Father, brought her to our door.

The woman from a town three hours away arrived in an old pick-up truck. A friend of hers had made the arrangements and had paid for her to come to Hidden Hollow for a personal retreat. Vincent looked out the window and said, "I can't believe that thing made it all the way here." Seconds later, smoke was pouring from underneath the hood, and antifreeze was running out. She was so embarrassed. We called AAA to haul it into town, and Vincent's mechanic friend will fix it over the weekend.

After things settled down, I saw her sitting outside in the front of the cross in a coat that was too thin. It made me cry.

Father, please bless this woman while she's here.

His Nearness

Monday, October 25, 2010, Groton Long Point, Connecticut
The foghorn just began sounding as the fog is thickening. Every once in a while, the sky will brighten and remind us that the sun is up there shining brightly somewhere. The foghorn reassures, comforts like your Holy Spirit. I can't see it, but I can hear it even when the fog is thick and murky. As the fog rolls in, I can no longer see the houses on the other side of the cove yet the sound of the horn is constant. It means the most when the fog is thickest.

Father, your nearness is sure and constant. I cannot see, but I trust you. O Father, guide my children and us safely home. Use the fog for your good purposes.

Monday, December 6, 2010, Flagstaff
I went to bed with such a heavy heart last night wondering how to handle a problem. I woke around 2 a.m. and was awake and tormented for hours wondering what I should do and say, running it over in my mind again and again.

In the wee hours, I looked at Vincent's form beneath the blanket. The Holy Spirit gave me the thought, "If I can do this, I can do anything." In other words, if He can bring Vincent and me together from either side of the continent, He can handle this problem.

I went back to sleep.

Hi Y'all

Our home sits at the end of a two-mile long, winding dirt road in the forest. When the children were young and on most school days, I would drive them to the bus stop at the end of the road in our large four-wheel drive vehicle which had a snow plow mounted on the front. Because we would frequently be running late and about to miss the bus, I would drive a little on the fast side. Okay, maybe a *lot* on the fast side, so much so that we would arrive careening around the last curve of the road in a cloud of dust with gravel flying. (Do not try this at home.) The bus driver had the audacity to suggest that we change our vehicle's personalized license plate from "Hi Y'all" to "Fly Y'all." As a result of my errant driving habits, my children have perpetuated the myth that I once hit 60 miles per hour on Hidden Hollow Road which, *of course*, is untrue. I mean, *that* speed would have resulted in "Bye Y'all!"

Nevertheless, in the interest of fairness and equal time, I include the following letter written years later by my daughter:

Saturday, April 16, 2011
Dear Mom,
More importantly, though, the other kids and I have your admission of speeding regularly IN WRITING! 60 mph on Hidden Hollow Road, 60 mph on Hidden Hollow Road...Oh, glorious day!
Love,
Shauna

Running

Tuesday, May 31, 2011, Groton Long Point

Last night I had a random thought while reading. The expression, "running out of time" makes me wonder if the "running" is the problem.

Sunday, August 14, 2011, Groton Long Point

Last night Caroline (two years old) was running on the deck at dusk. She didn't see the big step, and she ran over it. I cringed, and Shauna reached out, but no one could reach her in time. "Someone else" did. I couldn't believe my eyes. It was as if someone caught her under her arms and eased her down. Shauna and I both saw it. Unbelievable.

Life and Death

Saturday, September 17, 2011, Groton Long Point
   As I ponder beloved Aunt Theo's death[2], I think of how life on earth goes on as if no one has "left." It seems cruel and irreverent. Things should stop and take notice. That, I think, is one reason it is so important for the closest loved ones to do so. We need to consider what this life meant, and it helps us process that Theo has left although it doesn't feel real yet.

Sunday, September 18, 2011
Dear Family,
The very last Scripture I quoted at the end of Theo's message last week was, "To live is Christ and to die is gain." That is also the verse we are inscribing on the cornerstone of the chapel in Flagstaff, so it has been on my mind for both reasons.
This morning I went to our new little church here in Groton. The service hadn't started yet, and I was just enjoying the music while I looked out the huge windows in the front that overlook beautiful old trees. I decided I would find some of the day's readings in my Bible before the service started. I turned to the first one, Philippians 1:21 and read, "For to me, to live is Christ and to die is gain."
He does those little things. =)
Love,
Mom

---

2 See *Remembering Theo* in appendix.

Prayer for Protection

When a person has more to live for, they find they need less to live on.
Ken Shigematsu

Friday, October 27th, 2011, Flagstaff

I have been reading about the kings of Israel and how the things of the world could trip up even those who started out well. That could happen to anyone. Father, please protect us. I want to be like Isaiah who was rich in faith *and who remained faithful to God, undistracted, and of one mind. Father, may we be the same.*

Hidden Hollow Prayer Chapel

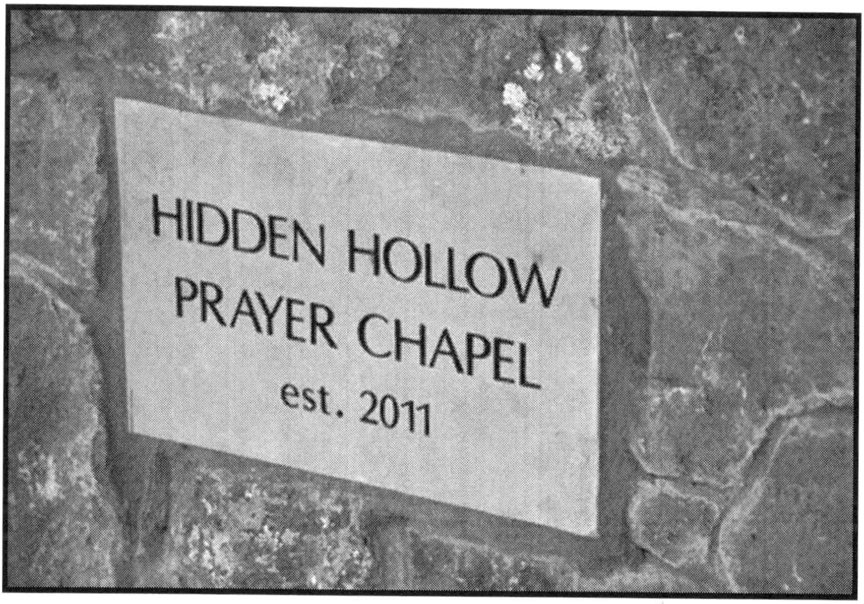
HIDDEN HOLLOW
PRAYER CHAPEL
est. 2011

Hidden Hollow Prayer Chapel

Wednesday, November 30, 2011, Flagstaff

As construction on the chapel progresses, one of the workers made a mistake and damaged the stained glass. We have been talking, praying, and wondering for weeks if we should leave the big window open to the forest. The view is so beautiful, but that window was meant for the stained glass! Is this you, Father? Please guide us.

I am sort of in disbelief that this accident happened shortly after I prayed about it. I so want the chapel to be conducive to prayer and worship, so I asked God to show us what to do. I have the wonderful feeling that God has taken us at our word and is going to make this little chapel His. It thrills me to no end to imagine what will happen inside those walls through the years! We are walking on holy ground. Hidden Hollow Prayer Chapel belongs to the Lord.

Thursday, December 1, 2011, Flagstaff

Well, we have decided that God has shown us to leave the chapel window open. It has been such a hard decision because the chapel was designed around the stained glass, and it is a beautiful piece. How this has all transpired is unbelievable. Remembering...

In 2000, after being asked to help create a small chapel for a hotel, I commissioned the stained glass artist. She chose the Scriptures and the theme for the stained glass: The Tree of Life. All of the Scriptures in the piece relate to trees in one way or another. Then, years later the two companion *pieces of calligraphy were penned using the verses from the glass, and the three pieces hung together in a Flagstaff church.*

Now the calligraphy will be placed on either side of the open chapel window. The Father knew where they would ultimately be placed permanently and what they would grace. All those beautiful verses about trees will be on either side of the window with a beautiful view of trees in the forest! His ways are too great for me!

Heartache

Saturday, July 7, 2012, Flagstaff

A little baby boy was born a few hours ago. He weighs one pound, six ounces. God bless Shannon, he called to tell us and said, "We have a son." Said the first forty-eight hours are critical.

My coffee is brewing, and it's dark outside. I can't sleep. After the first call came from Shannon that they were going to the operating room for the c-section, Vincent prayed through the night. I can't believe your timing, Father. You brought Vincent back from Connecticut at just the right time. Otherwise, I would be here alone. Thank you that he is here with me.

Christ, have mercy.

Welcome, little grandson.

Memorial Service for Weston Max

I am Becky Conti, Shauna's mother and Weston's grandmother. Shauna and Shannon have asked me to say a few words, and it is a privilege to do so.

The longer I live, the less I know. Have you ever felt that way? When I was twenty-five, I knew so much more than I know now. The things that remain, however, I am more convinced of than ever. And they are actually pretty simple.

First, life is hard. Life is hard. Jesus wasn't kidding when He said, "In this life you will have trouble." I don't have to give you examples because we all know this to be true. Some have it harder than others. We are broken people living in a broken world. Life is hard. *This* is hard.

But, there is more. This is not the full story. Life is hard, but God is good. And this is where I am hard-pressed to articulate what is inexpressible.

God is good, and He is *in* this with Shauna and Shannon. This is not psychological manipulation. This is not some general, sunny cheerfulness. Nor is it a benign, positive attitude which says, "Things are going to get better!" Because guess what? As the song says, "Life *is* hard, and it might *not* get easier."

No, when life hurts the most, like it does right now for Shauna and Shannon, this *of all times* is when they have experienced that abiding peace, that strong undercurrent which carries them. *This* is when they have experienced the peace that passes understanding.

It is a peace which *makes no sense*. And Shauna and Shannon would be the first to tell you that it doesn't come from them.

To the extent that words can describe the inexpressible, the following words shed some light, and these are words that have been precious to Shauna and Shannon during these last weeks and months.

Philippians 4:5: *The Lord is near.* Please hear that again. *The Lord is near. The Lord is near,* Shauna and Shannon. *Do not be anxious about anything, but in everything, by prayer and petition, giving thanks, present your requests to God. And the peace of God, which passes all understanding, will guard your hearts and your minds in Christ Jesus.*

There it is: *And the peace of God, which passes all understanding, will guard your hearts and your minds in Christ Jesus.*

Go figure.

When we hurt the most, God gives us a peace that really *does* pass understanding, and He is near.

And do you notice that hurting and peace are not mutually exclusive? Just because we experience peace from God does not mean that we do not hurt. And that is because we are human. Shauna and Shannon are hurting like crazy right now because they are human.

They are like jars of clay: fragile, subject to cracking and wearing thin.

II Corinthians 4:7 says, *...but there is a treasure in those jars of clay which shows that this all-surpassing power is from God and not from them.*

Please listen to those words again:

There is a treasure in those jars of clay which shows that this all-surpassing power is from God and not from them.

Shauna and Shannon are believers in Jesus Christ. We see the cycle of life all around us. Life, death, burial and resurrection in creation, in cultures and nations, throughout the world and repeatedly, over and over, in our own lives.

Just as Shauna and Shannon believe in the life, death, burial and resurrection of Jesus Christ, so we also see this in the life of Weston. He lived. He died. Today, he is buried. And we believe that he is resurrected in our Lord and Savior Jesus Christ.

The longer I live, the less I know. But, *this* I believe to be true.

Amen.

Phoenix, Arizona
August 1, 2012

Groton Long Point, Connecticut

Sad

Who we are on the other side of pain and loss is who we are at our best.

Joan Chittister

Monday, October 22, 2012, Groton Long Point
    Sad. I did not see this wave of grief coming. This is the week of Shauna's due date. We would have been so excited, and I would have been waiting for her phone call so I could go to Phoenix to help them. My heart aches. I didn't know I still had so much sadness inside.

Monday, November 5, 2012, Groton Long Point
    Today as I listened to worship music, I was wrapped up in the mystery—the not knowing, and it's okay. I'll never know or understand. I thought I did a long time ago because I was young.
    Truly, the longer I live, the less I know. And the mystery increases. For perhaps the first time in my life, I'm comfortable in this place.

Joy and Heartache Side by Side

Monday, November 19, 2012, Groton Long Point

And another grandson is born, this time to Natalie and Aaron. Yesterday Silas Wendell was born at home. He has lots of dark hair and is fairer than Jude. When I talked to two-year-old Jude, he said, "The special baby is purple."

The View from Home

Fresh Rosemary and a Thorn

Monday, February 18, 2013, Flagstaff
    Simple joys are a blessing from your hand, Father. A good night's sleep. Coffee and quiet this morning. Napping this afternoon with Vincent nearby. A dinner of delicious roasted chicken with fresh rosemary and roasted fresh roots. I am a blessed woman.

Thursday, February 28, 2013, Flagstaff
    The thorn in my side. As I thought about (and experienced) my constant fatigue the other day, I thought of an image that describes it.
    All of my life I have walked alongside family and friends, but it is as though they are walking on the ground while I am walking in a swimming pool next to them. We can certainly see one another and accompany each other, but I can't keep up. I'm having to work much harder to walk through the water. My legs tire, but I keep trying. I want to be with them. When we reach our destination, I am worn out just getting there, and once there it is hard to enjoy it. I am already spent.
    The last part is the saddest. So many experiences end up just being an exercise in endurance for me. It is all about pacing myself, on which I am the expert.

All that to say, Father, you have blessed me and provided for me. I have great health otherwise. Help me, once again, to embrace my weaknesses. May you be glorified through them, Father. "Your strength is made perfect in our weakness." Use them for good. Amen.

My Presence will go with you, and I will give you rest. Ex. 33:14

Be Still

March, 2013, Flagstaff

I was meditating on Psalm 46:10, "Be still and know that I am God," and a paraphrase occurred to me which was, "Be still so that I can know that you are God."

How to Think

Wednesday, July 10, 2013, Flagstaff

Last week Vincent and I were chatting with a man I have known for years. Something came up about my children and how our family has a variety of political views. He said with a smile, "Becky, didn't you teach your kids *what* to think?" I responded, "I didn't teach my kids *what* to think. I taught them *how* to think," and poked him in the ribs.

Weaning

There is treasure buried in the field of every one of our days,
even the bleakest or dullest, and it is our business,
as we journey, to keep our eyes peeled for it.
                                            Frederick Buechner

Monday, September 30, 2013 (my sixty-second birthday), Groton Long Point
   As of late, I have sensed that God is growing me up by weaning me from the constant sense of His nearness, much as a mother leaves a child's room so the baby will sleep. The baby frets, but the mother knows it is necessary, and she watches from the partly cracked door.
   I, too, "fought" this for a time. No longer. I know He is, and I know He is with me even as from the baby's perspective, I can't see Him. May I learn these lessons well and increase in wisdom.
   So, I pray not from a place of passionate emotions or intense "God experiences" but from the place of trust in my unseen Lord. It is a quiet trust that is preceded by decades of the other.

Seasons

Monday, October 21, 2013, Groton Long Point

I drove to New Britain and back this weekend. The trees along the road are on fire! It is lined with red maples, the leaves gold and orange, which is still startling to a girl from the southwest.

I am in the autumn of my life. You have taught me so much, Father, and you continue to reveal things to me. My colors (lessons learned) are deep, possibly at their most beautiful as long as I don't become bitter by looking back and longing for what was. If I do that, I miss today. Perhaps others can be blessed by those colors. That is what I want. Father, help me cherish and truly enjoy this rich season.

During winter, old age, I expect there will be hidden gifts. The cold snow requires the land to rest from its labors. There is important "work" being done beneath the snow, which is necessary. Life's winter season is, perhaps, the season to be still and know that He is God, to ponder and to pray. Then, after that season, we are able to present to God a heart of wisdom—a gift He will cherish.

Crooked Tree

Home

Saturday, January 25, 2014, Flagstaff
 Back and forth. We are back from Connecticut.
 When I think of our family's move to Hidden Hollow nearly twenty-five years ago, I am surprised. It was a circuitous route going from Dallas to Sedona with no consideration of Flagstaff. We ended up here only to shorten the commute for work.
 Father, thank you for this beautiful little piece of land and for the way it has blessed people over the years. It is one of the prettiest spots in the state. Use it to bless your children.
 My longing is for an eternal home, and nothing on this earth will ever satisfy completely, not even the sweet smell of ponderosa pines. I wonder, after we die, if we take a breath for the first time in heaven, smell the air and say, "Ahh... This is home. This is what I had always longed for."

Quaking Aspen

Abundance

God love it.

Sunday, June 15, 2014, Flagstaff

On Friday night Marcus, our beloved drummer, proposed to Kari. He texted all of us and wrote, "She said yes!"

Tuesday, June 17, 2014, Flagstaff

Preston is on tour with his band, celebrating his thirtieth birthday on the road, and doing what he loves most, making music.

Wednesday, June 25, 2014, Flagstaff

The forest teems with life: insects, birds, fox, rabbits, squirrels, chipmunks, skunks, pocket gophers, deer, a bear. Even before it reaches us, I can hear the wind in the ponderosas as it works its way toward us. The soil, the curved earth is lush and nourishing. Sacred ground in which the Father delights. One small window.

Friday, July 4, 2014, Flagstaff

Today, (today!) Natalie and Aaron's family moves from New York City to Flagstaff, where they will raise their family among the ponderosa pines and quaking aspen.

Morning

Saturday, July 5, 2014, Phoenix

It was a sacred night. Shauna's labor was long and hard. I sensed God's presence so strongly. He seemed to inhabit the room and hover. In early morning William Andrew was born healthy and beautiful. He calmed as soon as he was laid on Shauna's chest.

Shannon, Shauna, Natalie and I all wept tears of bittersweet joy.

Weeping may endure for a night, but joy comes in the morning.
Psalm 30:5

APPENDIX

Remembering Theo

Theo Pauline Campbell White. She was something, wasn't she? And, she had more nicknames than anyone I've ever known: FleeBo, The Beehive, Mom, Granny Grunt, Graneer, Aunt Theo, Great Grandma and the one that stuck, See-More.

Theo was born February 4, 1925 in Zwolle, Louisiana, to Harrison and Lillie Pearl Young Campbell. She was the seventh of eight children to survive to adulthood. She grew up during the Great Depression in a small, rural southern town. She lived through the horrors of World War II, and in the midst of that war she met John B. White, a Nebraskan, who was stationed at Fort Polk, Louisiana. Theo became one of thousands of war brides when they married on August 29, 1942. Following the war, they moved to McCool Junction, Nebraska, where they spent the next 62 years working and raising a family. The rest is history.

The time and place of Theo's early life is merely history to some of us. We have only read about it in books or studied it in history classes. But, many refer to hers as The Greatest Generation. They learned the valuable lessons of sacrifice and perseverance *because* of the war and the depression. They have been our examples and our mentors. Their lives, their stories have so much to teach us. Besides, after they are gone that leaves the Baby Boomers, my generation, as the elders and examples which is *really* a scary thought! I don't think so! My generation spent way too many years in a purple haze.

Think of the ways in which the world has changed in the course of Theo's 86 years. Several months ago LaMoine happened to mention that she had gotten a malt for Theo, so the next time I talked to Theo I mentioned it. That reminded her of a memory, and she told me a little story that gives us a glimpse into her early years.

Using her words she said, "Young people today would not understand what my brothers and sisters and I had for malts when I was a child. We would put milk in a jug and screw the top on tight. Then, we would put the jug in a tub of ice and roll it around until it got sort of frothy. People today wouldn't think much of it, but to us it tasted good." Can you imagine how a simple thing like cold, frothy milk would taste to a little girl on a hot summer's day in Louisiana? It is a picture of a different time.

Just like you, I have hundreds of memories of Theo. My very first and earliest memory of Theo was when I was a very little girl visiting here in McCool. John, Theo, Johnny and LaMoine lived in the white house with the front porch. I always loved that porch. I do not know how old I was, but I must have been very young because I was playing on the floor crawling under the kitchen table, in and around the chairs like it was a maze as very small children will do. Theo was ironing, and a woman stopped by to visit. They sipped coffee and talked which was an everyday occurrence for homemakers in the 1950s.

What do you think they were talking about? Their families? The news? No, they talked that morning for what seemed a very long time about the Lord, about faith. As a matter of fact, I would go somewhere else in the house, come back and they were still at it. I did not hear everything they said, and I certainly did not understand it all, but I could tell that God, that Theo's relationship with God, was very important to her. It made an impression on me that I have never forgotten. Theo was a good woman.

Another memory was the station, White's Service Station. What a picture of a small American family business, a family that worked together for years. John and Johnny working on cars and pumping gas, the cranes, Theo cooking in the cafe' and LaMoine waiting tables. Like many of you, I have a lot of memories of Theo in that place. For example, I remember her talking about her recipe for the meat loaf she served. That's a classic American dish I don't hear of often any more. During those years, I suspect we did not realize how very special it was, a family working together like that. Now, years later we look back on that with nostalgia and appreciate its unique place in our American culture.

Another wonderful memory and one that was repeated over and over was the number of hours I spent in the back seats of cars on road trips or in small private planes with Theo, my family, Johnny and LaMoine or some combination thereof. Theo and my mother would give us bologna sandwiches made with Miracle Whip on Wonder Bread. Remember how Wonder Bread would stick to the roof of your mouth? We kids would sit in the back playing, looking out the windows, poking and scratching all the way across the country.

Do you remember the song, "Get Your Kicks on Route 66?" Well, I *literally* got my kicks on Route 66. "Why?" you may ask. Well, I was sitting next to Theo's daughter who shall remain unnamed at this point. I think I still have a scar on my shin from one of those trips. And Theo, with her dead-pan expression, would come up with these one-liners that would send my mother into fits of laughter. And, there we were making memories mile-after-mile.

No matter how long and tiring the trip was it was all worth it when we got to Theo's house. Still a southern girl at heart, she could make a mean pot of black-eyed peas and a great pan of cornbread. My favorite, however, was her pot roast. Honestly, Theo made the best I have ever tasted. And then, there was her carrot cake, and she would always have a pot of coffee ready for company. Theo was a good woman.

Theo had gifts that blessed all of us and many more besides. For one, she had the ability to live in the present. What I mean by that is the way she would drink in the present moment. When she was with you, *she was with you*. When she was looking at creation, a bird or the sunset or a simple flower, you got the feeling that she was really *seeing* which, of course, is why she was nicknamed See-More. Because, she did not miss a thing.

In those moments, and there were hundreds of them, she was not looking around for something else to do. She never gave the impression that she was ready to move on to the next thing. She took great joy in the moment, and that is a rare gift, especially in a world with so many distractions.

And then, there was her love of people, and oh my, how she loved people. She loved them, us, so well. Didn't you love the way she said your name, the way she called you, "Honey"? She listened, and she loved. It was not a passive love but an active, intentional love. She never forgot her family scattered coast-to-coast, north to south. She loved them with all her heart, and she stayed in touch. She loved John B and was a faithful wife. And, she loved you, Johnny, LaMoine, your children and grandchildren with all of her heart. And, she still had love left over for all the rest of us!

Of course, I am not telling you anything you did not know and experience. She had a very special gift. When you were with her, you felt cherished and treasured. You felt like she saw something special in you. And, you know what? She did! She had an insight into people, a sixth sense that was uncanny. She would meet a person, and later she would tell you what she sensed. She was nearly always right. That does not mean Theo put blinders on. She knew I was imperfect. She knew you were imperfect, but she loved us anyway. Unconditionally. She saw the best in people, and that is what she focused on.

I keep a journal, and several months ago I jotted down something she said. It was, "We shouldn't judge others. You never know how much hurt they have, and you hope that later on they'll do right."

She did not only *hope* for us; she *prayed* for us. There is no telling the countless prayers she whispered for you and me and many more over the years. Theo was a good woman.

Of course, she had an incredible love of children, and she was just a natural. Her house could be full of kids making noise, making messes, running in and out slamming doors, and she would just cruise right along with all the chaos. She loved the little ones, as she called them. That love never ran out, and we loved her back, didn't we?

And finally, Theo loved the Lord. Remember the conversation I overheard from underneath the kitchen table? Well, that was a constant theme in Theo's life. She was a true believer, and she loved Him. Oh my, how she loved Him.

You know, when times get tough we often see the true colors of a person, and that was certainly the case as Theo's health failed. There is a beautiful verse in II Corinthians 4. It says, "Therefore, we do not lose heart, but though our outer man is decaying, yet our inner man is being renewed day-by-day."

That verse explains what was happening to Theo during her last months. Her body was dying, but her inner spirit was being renewed. Her physical health was failing, but her inner spirit was being made new again. And, that is why she...was...not...afraid...to...die. That is why she could say over and over and over, "We have so much to be thankful for." We would talk about God's faithfulness, and she would say, "Oh my yes, He is right here with me, and I talk to Him."

There was no bitterness or anger toward God. What was present was the same love of God and people that had always been there. As the things of earth grew dim for Theo, the things of God shone brighter. She was on the way home. She knew that God is real, and she experienced His love and His presence. It can be the same for you and me.

Ecclesiastes, chapter 3, begins with these words: "For everything there is a season, and a time for every matter under heaven: a time to be born and a time to die."

As hard as it is for us to say goodbye to Theo, it was time. And, do you want to know the wonderful news? The great news? Dying is not the end of the world. Death is not the end of the world. Theo was born. She lived, and she died. Today, she is buried, and she will be resurrected in her Lord and Savior, Jesus Christ.

Death is called the last enemy in Scripture, and there are some amazing words about death in I Corinthians 15. The Apostle Paul writes, "Death has been swallowed up in victory. Where O death, is your victory?

Where O death, is your sting?" The Apostle is almost taunting death. It is like he is saying, "Show me your stuff, death! Come on, where is your punch? Where is your sting?"

And, the answer to that question? Death has no victory. The last enemy has been defeated. The shadow of death passed over Theo, but it cannot destroy her because death does not have the last word. Jesus Christ has the last word.

He said, "I am the resurrection and the life. He who believes in me will live, even though he dies; and whoever lives and believes in me will never die."

And, that is why we can say that death is not the end of the world. Theo knew this, and she experienced it.

Nevertheless, on this side, saying goodbye is hard, and that is why we gather together. We need the love and comfort of one another. We stop to remember the life and death of Theo because her life mattered to God, because she made a difference in your life and mine and because she made a difference in the world and in eternity. The world is a better place because Theo lived.

And now, a few words to those closest to her:

Thelma, you were her sister and best friend for life. What a gift you were to one another.

Hayden and Erin, your great grandma loved you, and you delighted her.

Mandy, Ginger, Ryan and Amber, she sang your praises! As she was wrapping up her time on earth, she told me several times, "You know, not one of my grandchildren has ever been in serious trouble." Can't you just hear her saying that? She was so proud of you, and wow she loved you.

Johnny and LaMoine, along with John B, you were the loves of her life.

Johnny, she always delighted in your intelligence and sense of humor. After your last trip to see her, she said, "Johnny would sit in this room and drink coffee and we'd visit. Ooh, I love Johnny." And, she knew you loved her.

LaMoine, to simply say you blessed her life is grossly inadequate. She was so grateful for the many sacrifices you made for her. You have completed the race for and with your mother, and we are all so grateful. As you know, she repeatedly said, "I don't know what I would do without LaMoine. She and Bob mean so much to me."

And there is one more. Bob, if there were an award for the best son-in-law in the world it would go to you. What a loyal son-in-law you have been for 45 years. When she talked about all you had done, she would always start by saying, "Bob, God bless him, did such-and-such for me today."

In one of my conversations with Theo in March, she was counting her blessings, and she said, "There's a lot of goodness in this ole' world, and I have a wonderful, wonderful family."

We do not know a lot about heaven, but there are some hints in the Bible. My favorite one is that there will be no more tears.

The cycle of life: life, death, burial and resurrection. *To live is Christ, and to die is gain.* And, Theo has now reached the best part of all.

Amen.

Rebecca Biegert Conti
McCool Junction, Nebraska
September 10, 2011

Hidden Hollow Prayer Chapel Dedication

Vincent and I are *glad* you are here. Thank you so much for coming on this snowy day to the dedication of Hidden Hollow Prayer Chapel.

It is very meaningful to us that you all come from a variety of traditions. It makes this gathering so rich to have Mennonites, Catholics, Pentecostals, people from mainline denominations, conservative evangelicals and progressive evangelicals all under the roof of this little chapel.

We are here for one reason: because of Jesus Christ whose resurrection we just celebrated a week ago. And, today, we are united by Him.

As you know, Jesus often left the cities with his disciples and would go to a quiet place to pray. He is our example, and that is what we do here at Hidden Hollow Prayer Retreat. We make available a quiet place for people to pray and rest. Isaiah 28:12 says, "This is the resting place. Let the weary rest," and that is our mission.

This little chapel is a continuation of that purpose. It is also an answer to prayer and a dream-come-true. I would like to introduce a few people who have had a part in its creation.

First, Mike Furr is here with his wife, Ellen. Mike and his crew built this chapel using native stone for the exterior. He is known for the quality of his work, and he also has the eye of an artist. He suggested many of the beautiful touches that enhance the interior. Thanks to Mike we expect this chapel to be standing for a long, long time. It is meaningful to have a long-time neighbor and friend do the actual construction.

Next is our friend, Jan Petrucci. She is a talented calligrapher and teacher who lettered these two stunning pieces of calligraphy you see adorning the window. Each piece is her rendering of the Scripture verses around the theme of a tree or trees. The meditative quality of her art is astounding.

And finally, we have Gabe Furr. Gabe is Mike and Ellen's son. He and his brother, Dan, grew up here on Hidden Hollow Road and were childhood friends with my two sons. Gabe is a talented artist and sculptor, and he designed, welded and installed the beautiful Celtic cross on the outside roof of the chapel.

We are grateful to all three of these friends for helping bring this dream to pass.

And, today we dedicate it to the Lord. We give it back to Him. We are setting this chapel apart for prayer and worship.

Psalm 22:3 says that God inhabits our praises, and we believe that. Inhabit means to dwell within. So, even when we are hurting, even when life is hard, when we offer a sacrifice of prayer, God is glorified and we are comforted. It is one of the mysteries of our faith. We also believe that God hears, listens and answers our prayers, and that is the other piece. This chapel is a place to rest, to worship and to pray.

We ask God to meet people within these walls. We ask that people who walk in these doors will experience His love and His presence. We ask God to comfort, strengthen and bless the many who will come here.

We commit it to Him in the Name of the Father, the Son and the Holy Spirit. And, we pray that it will stand as a testimony to Him for a very long time – long after we have left this earth.

Rebecca Biegert Conti
Hidden Hollow
April 14, 2012

A Contemplation of the Table of Grace

Communion Service

Tonight we have prepared for you a contemplation of the table of grace. To contemplate means to focus on, to dwell upon, to meditate on. In order for you to have that opportunity, it means that rather than fill our time and space together, we are going to open up time and space for you. I encourage you to inhabit the quiet, relax, enjoy it and rest in it.

One result of such contemplation is that rather than working hard to master the Scripture passages, we allow the Scriptures to master *us*. Let's begin by listening to these words from Luke 23:39-43 which were spoken at the time Jesus hung on the cross with the two thieves.

> One of the criminals who hung there hurled insults at Him: "Aren't you the Christ! Save yourself and us!" But the other criminal rebuked him. "Don't you fear God," he said, "since you are under the same sentence? We are punished justly, for we are getting what our deeds deserve. But this man has done nothing wrong."

> Then he said, "Lord, remember me when you come into your kingdom." Jesus answered him, "I tell you the truth, today you will be with me in paradise."

These are some of the words of Jesus, spoken on the night of the last supper (Matthew 26:28-29)

> This is the blood of the covenant, which is poured out for many for the forgiveness of sins. I tell you, I will not drink of this fruit of the vine from now on until that day when I drink it anew with you in my Father's kingdom.

I am the parent of four adult children. All four of them have grown up and left home. Some of them live very far from my home in Flagstaff, and some live as close as Phoenix.

When they plan to come home for a visit, I anticipate their arrival. I put fresh sheets on their beds and get rid of the cobwebs in their rooms. Most of the planning, however, goes into the meal we share upon their homecoming. I plan the menu, buy the groceries and fix their favorite dishes.

Now, my husband enjoys and is a much better cook than I am. As a matter of fact, when he took over our kitchen, it was one of the happiest days of my life! But, I can make a mean pot of homemade chicken and dumplings, which is one of Marcus' favorites.

When I stew the chicken and season it just so, it smells scrumptious. Then, I mix the dumpling batter and plop it gently into the stew. It bubbles until the dumplings are as light as air, and the rich stew simmers underneath.

As I am preparing it, it smells so good, and I know it tastes good, but I wait. I wait until my son has arrived. It wouldn't make sense to eat it beforehand, would it? Why? Well, because I want to enjoy it *with him*. I want to celebrate his homecoming. I have planned and worked, but it is not just about the food. It is an occasion, and I can't wait to sit around the table with him laughing, talking, basking in his presence and enjoying the food. It is a celebration.

Did you know that Jesus is doing the same thing? He is waiting for us. He is anticipating our arrival in His Father's kingdom. He is planning and preparing, and He tells us that He is saving the wine for our arrival. He isn't going to drink it without us. He wants to enjoy it *with us*.

Imagine that! Our Savior, Jesus Christ, is waiting for us! Just as I enjoy watching my son enjoy the meal I have prepared for him, Jesus can't wait to see the expression on our faces when we take that first sip. I have a feeling the wine He has prepared for us is going to be very good, just like the wine He made at the wedding in Cana. Yes, it will be pure and delicious, but I think that what is going to make it so sweet to Him is that we will be drinking it *together* with Him. His waiting will be over. For those of us who may have substance abuse issues now, there will be no more brokenness of that sort or of any other sort. We will drink the wine with Him, and it will be pure joy.

By the way, guess who else is going to be there? The thief on the cross. Jesus said he would be.

In the meantime, here on earth, He has asked us to drink the wine and eat the bread as we remember His death for us. He did it for us, and He wants us to remember.

> On the night that He was betrayed, Jesus took bread, gave thanks and broke it, and gave it to his disciples, saying, "Take and eat; this is my body." Then he took the cup, gave thanks and offered it to them, saying, "Drink from it, all of you. This is my blood of the covenant, which is poured out for many for the forgiveness of sins. I tell you, I will not drink of this fruit of the vine from now on until that day when I drink it anew with you in my Father's kingdom." Matthew 26:26-29

Go now, secure in the knowledge that *you are loved* by your heavenly Father. Remembering all that Jesus Christ has done for you, rejoice! He has set us free!

Rebecca Biegert Conti
Flagstaff, Arizona
June 15, 2006

The Upside-Down Kingdom

Palm Sunday

The title of this message, The Upside-Down Kingdom, is not original with me. About 25 years ago, Kraybill wrote a book with this title which has now become somewhat of a classic.

It's Palm Sunday, the day we remember Jesus' triumphal entry into the city of Jerusalem. What you see scattered on the floor is a reminder of what the people did when He entered the city. They threw their coats down before him in an expression of welcome and honor. They threw palm branches down and waved them in the air in an expression of great joy and worship.

Let's read about this incredible scene in John 12:12-19:

"The next day the great crowd that had come for the Feast heard that Jesus was on his way to Jerusalem. They took palm branches and went out to meet him, shouting, 'Hosanna! Blessed is he who comes in the name of the Lord! Blessed is the King of Israel!' Jesus found a young donkey and sat upon it, as it is written, 'Do not be afraid, O Daughter of Zion; see, your king is coming, seated on a donkey's colt.' At first his disciples did not understand all this. Only after Jesus was glorified did they realize that these things had been written about him and that they had done these things to him.

Now the crowd that was with him when he called Lazarus from the tomb and raised him from the dead continued to spread the word. Many people, because they had heard that he had given this miraculous sign went out to meet him. So, the Pharisees said to one another, 'See, this is getting us nowhere. Look how the whole world has gone after him!'"

Let's unpack this. Starting with verse 12, "The next day the great crowd that had come for the Feast heard that Jesus was on his way to Jerusalem." Jesus was a *very controversial figure*. At this time, Jerusalem had a permanent population of 80,000. Thousands of people had already arrived in Jerusalem for the Feast of the Passover. The population swelled anywhere from 100,000 to 250,000 during Passover. There was an excitement in the air. They had waited an entire year for this, and it was the highlight of their year.

Now previously, Jesus had raised Lazarus from the dead in the town of Bethany. He had a following there and, as a result, a crowd was already following Him and the disciples as they made their way from Bethany. Word spread into the walled city of Jerusalm that Jesus was on His way. And, before you know it, the crowd from Bethany meets up with the crowd that rushes outside the city walls to greet Jesus, and *there is a scene!*

Verse 13 says, "They took palm branches and went out to meet him, shouting, "Hosanna! Blessed is he who comes in the name of the Lord. Blessed is the King of Israel!"

Hosanna means, "Save us!" They are shouting, "Save us! Save us!" From whom do you think they want Jesus to save them? From Rome, of course, the brutal occupying forces of Rome.

Then they shout, "Blessed is he who comes in the name of the Lord! Blessed is the King of Israel!" They are praising Him. They are recognizing Him as the King of Israel. They are worshipping and rejoicing.

Now, this is significant for many reasons, but first I want to mention timing. Timing is everything, it appears, and *it was time* for this to happen. But prior to this day, things were different. Jesus had been trying to keep a lid on things. For example, in John 2:4 we see Jesus at the wedding in Cana. Jesus' mother told him, "They have no more wine." Jesus responded, "My time has not yet come."

In Mark 8:30, Jesus asks the disciples, "Who do you say that I am?" Peter answers, "You are the Christ." And, how does Jesus respond? He warns them not to tell anyone about Him.

Lastly, in Luke 8:51, Jesus went to the house of Jairus because they thought their daughter had died. Jesus healed her, and her parents were astounded. What did He tell them? "Do not tell *anyone* what happened."

But, today is different. Jesus is going public. He is allowing the people to shout their praises and thanksgiving. He is allowing the people to worship Him publicly. It is the first time He basically says, "Cut loose! *It is time.*"

Jesus' entry into Jerusalem was Jesus' announcement that, "The hour had come for the Son of Man to be glorified."

Now, we look at verse 14 which says, "Jesus found a young donkey and sat upon it, as it is written, 'Do not be afraid, O Daughter of Zion; see your king is coming seated on a donkey's colt.'"

John, the author, tells us this so we know the fashion in which Jesus arrived in Jerusalem. This verse is addressed to the city of Jerusalem, which is what "Daughter of Zion" means. It is saying, "Jerusalem, don't be afraid. Here He comes! You'll know it's Him. He'll be on a donkey's colt."

This verse was a prophecy, written 500 years earlier and recorded in Zechariah 9:9. Every little detail, every little piece of this scene has significance. And, the manner in which Jesus rode into Jerusalem says enormous things about Jesus and His kingdom. It has enormous significance for you and me.

Normally, when kings and military warriors entered the great city of Jerusalem, things were quite different. They usually rode a war horse or a wheeled vehicle. They carried a sword and wore a crown. There was great pomp and circumstance. The spoils of their conquest, gold, treasures, conquered people, were displayed for the people to see. I would imagine there was a look of great pride and victory on their faces, a proud countenance and posture.

Then came Jesus, the King of all these other kings, and how does He arrive? On a young donkey, on a donkey which is a sign of peace. He did not come as a conqueror but as a messenger of peace. He rode not on a royal steed but on a donkey. He did not arrive with a royal entourage which was brightly adorned, but he arrived with *common people* who laid down their only coats for the donkey to walk over. He did not arrive with the blare of trumpets or loud pronouncements proclaiming his arrival, but he arrived with the *common people* shouting their praises.

He did not arrive with great banners or shining swords catching and reflecting the sun's rays, but he arrived with the common people breaking branches off wherever they could find them and waving those. He arrived in humility, without pomp and ceremony.

Every little detail in this scene has significance. It is packed with meaning. And, what does His manner of arrival say about Him and the kingdom of heaven?

Well, it tells us it is unlike any other kingdom in all the world. It is an upside-down kingdom. It is not like the others. This king comes offering peace in all its many dimensions. This king says the least shall be the greatest. This king says if you lose your life for His sake, you will gain your life. This king says if you try to save your life, you will lose it. This king says he came to serve, not to be served. This king lays down his life for us, and you can add many more of these paradoxes. Start by taking a look at the Sermon on the Mount. This king, in His own words, is *gentle and humble*. This king is ushering in the upside-down kingdom.

Let's look at the people in this remarkable scene. First we come to the disciples, his best friends, his companions. Verse 26 says this, "At first his disciples did not understand all this. Only after Jesus was glorified did they realize that these things had been written about him and that they had done these things to him."

Can you imagine their confusion? First, when Jesus told them it was time to go to Jerusalem? They probably couldn't believe their ears! They knew Jerusalem was dangerous for Jesus. They might have thought, "What is he thinking? He's walking into a death trap!" And...He...was. And, He knew it. He knew that the jubilant crowd declaring him King was going to take Him straight to the cross.

This was all the jealous, threatened Pharisees needed to hear. They panicked and thought, "Look, how the whole world has gone after Him."

And, the people who were shouting Hosanna? They think He is going to free them from Rome. They think Jesus is a political and military Messiah. I guess we could say they missed the message that the donkey was a sign of *peace*.

The disciples are confused and afraid, the Pharisees are mistaken, and the common people have missed the message. If this scene were not so passionate, so tragic, we might say it was a comedy of errors.

This sounds like someone I know. Myself. Missing the point. I am just like these people, all of them, and maybe you are, too.

Verse 16 says the disciples did not understand until after the fact. This is the story of my life. I love this verse because it tells me *that I'm not the only one*. Half the time I have no or little clue what God is doing. I miss what He's doing or saying until after the fact. But then quite often, I look back and say, "Ah ha! Now, I see what He was doing! Now, I get it!" But at the time, I am clueless. At other times, just like the masses that day, I see one thing when God is really doing something quite different. I see Jesus riding a donkey, and I think, "Yea, man. He's gonna bust some heads!" Again, I am clueless until after the fact, until time has given me some perspective and the hindsight of 20-20 vision.

Steve Brown says this, "Whatever you think God is doing in your life, there is a very good possibility that He isn't. God's ways are circuitous. He is more interested in letting you be a part of what He is doing than He is in telling us what he is doing."

This used to frustrate and trouble me, but I no longer despair over my cluelessness. The Christian journey is a walk by faith, not by sight. For one thing, I know Jesus gets me. He knows I'm human, that I don't understand and that I become confused. But most importantly, I don't despair over my lack of understanding because the disciples' lack of understanding did not derail Jesus' mission. Neither can my human-ness derail God's plans.

I know this because of a tiny little verse in Job. Job 42:2 says, "I know, God, that you can do all things; no plan of yours can be thwarted."

We stress and worry so much about *getting it right* as if the whole thing, whatever that is, depends solely on us, as if it's all about us! Friends, God is bigger than our lack of understanding just as He was on the day of Jesus' triumphal entry into Jerusalem. God is bigger than our poor choices, just as He was when Judas betrayed Jesus. God is bigger than our wrong turns just as He was when Peter denied Him. God is bigger than the government or religious leaders who are powerful and corrupt, just as He was in the week that followed the triumphal entry and preceded His crucifixion.

The salvation of the world hung in the balance. The death, burial and resurrection of Jesus was about to change everything, and no one could thwart that.

God is not bound by our lack of understanding, our poor choices, our wrong turns, bad government or corrupt religion. We do the best we can to discern and understand, and we seek godly counsel. And then, we need to give ourselves a break, and take the burden off our shoulders, a burden we were never meant to bear. Job 42:2 says, "I know that you can do all things; no plan of yours can be thwarted."

Friend, when we look at Jesus' triumphal entry in that light, it tells me it is not about us! It's about Him! And although Jesus was surrounded by thousands of people who were praising Him, the sobering truth is that He was utterly alone on that day in that only He knew fully what it meant and what was really going on.

About that day, Blaise Pascal says this, "Jesus is alone on earth, not merely with no one to feel and share his agony, but with no one even to know of it. Heaven and he are the only ones to know."

Jesus said many things by the way He entered Jerusalem that day, about the kind of king He is, about the kingdom of heaven, the *upside-down* kingdom of heaven. And even though the people did not understand what was really going on, Jesus accepted their praise, their broken hallelujahs because *it was time.*

How does one respond to this? How do our hearts, minds and lives respond? Well first, we join the multitude, and we praise and worship Him saying, "Hosanna! Save us! Save us! Blessed is he who comes in the name of the Lord! Blessed is the King of Israel!"

Then, we remember that, like the disciples, we very often won't "get it" until after the fact, but that even our lack of understanding cannot derail God's purposes.

Next, we ponder this amazing, unbelievable, wonderful, mysterious upside-down kingdom, what this says about the kind of savior He is, what this says about what God is like, and what this means for us.

And our response? Look again at the coats and branches the people threw on the roadway. Ponder what it means to fully participate in this upside-down kingdom, and listen to these words by Andrew of Crete:

"So it is ourselves that we must spread under Christ's feet, not coats or lifeless branches or shoots of trees, matter which wastes away and delights the eye only for a few brief hours. But we have clothed ourselves with Christ's grace, with the whole Christ – 'for as many of you as were baptized into Christ have put on Christ' – so let us spread ourselves like coats under his feet."

Amen.

Rebecca Biegert Conti
Flagstaff, Arizona
March 28, 2010

Life, Death, Burial & Resurrection

Easter Sunday

*Easter...It is almost too brilliant for me to contemplate;
it is like looking directly into the sun; I am
burned and blinded by life.*

Madeleine L'Engle

He is risen! He is risen indeed!

As you know well, today is the highlight of the Christian calendar. Christians around the world are remembering the story of the resurrection of Jesus Christ, and Christians around the world are celebrating this resurrection. They are hearing the familiar Scriptures once again, and even though we have heard the story over and over and over, we want to hear it again. We NEED to hear it again. We need to be reminded of what it means for you, for me and for the world because we're all in this together.

Before we read the verses about the resurrection, let's remember what came before, what happened in real time on middle eastern soil, a true story from our world's ancient history.

Jesus of Nazareth had been preaching, teaching and healing people. He had been living and preaching a revolutionary message that did not sit well with the Pharisees who were the religious leaders of that day. People were flocking to Him to hear his stories, to be healed. They sensed something in Him that they had never experienced before. He even sought out and loved the outcasts, the people the religious leaders shunned.

Jesus was a great teacher, but *there's more*. Jesus healed people of all sorts of problems. T*here's more*. Jesus was even a prophet who could tell people about their pasts and what was to come even though He had never met them before. And, *there's more*. Jesus loved all types of people, and He loved them well. *There's more*.

Of all the things Jesus did and of all the things Jesus said, there is the one that was the most shocking of all. We need to sit down for this one. *He said He was God's Son and that He and the Father were one.*

That is what blew the lid off the Pharisees' heads. They were already threatened by the people flocking to hear him. They were jealous of the people's affection for Him, and they felt their power over the people slipping away, But, what really did it was when He said He was the Son of God. That was it! They considered it blasphemy, and He must die.

And…He…did…die.

They tortured Him and killed Him using a cruel, inhumane method of execution. They hung Him on a cross made of wood on which He would die of asphyxiation.

Now, we know from history that the Romans killed thousands of Jews by this method. Jesus was not the only one. There were roadways lined with crosses on which hung condemned criminals. Jesus was one of thousands of Jews who were executed.

But, there was something different about Jesus of Nazareth. He was not like the others. You see, if this were the end of the story, if he had been executed, died and buried like the others, we probably would never have even heard His name.

Those who actually knew Him would have said that He was a great teacher, that He healed people, maybe even that He was a prophet. But, they certainly would not have believed His claim to be God's son, would they? And, all these years later, we would read about the execution of thousands and thousands of Jews in our history books. But, we probably would never have heard of Jesus of Nazareth. Because if this were the end of the story, He would just have been one more unfortunate Jew to die at the hands of a cruel Roman empire.

But, this is not the end of the story. *There is more.* Let's read what happened three days after He died:

Matthew 28:1-10 says, "After the Sabbath, at dawn on the first day of the week, Mary Magdalene and the other Mary went to look at the tomb. There was a violent earthquake, for an angel of the Lord came down from heaven and, going to the tomb, rolled back the stone and sat on it. His appearance was like lightning, and his clothes were white as snow. The guards were so afraid of him that they shook and became like dead men. The angel said to the women, 'Do not be afraid, for I know that you are looking for Jesus, who was crucified. He is not here; he has risen just as he said. Come and see the place where he lay. Then go quickly and tell his disciples: 'He has risen from the dead and is going ahead of you into Galilee. There you will see him.' Now I have told you.' So the women hurried away from the tomb, afraid yet filled with joy, and ran to tell his disciples. Suddenly Jesus met them, 'Greetings,' he said. They came to him, clasped his feet and worshipped him. Then Jesus said to them, 'Do not be afraid. Go and tell my brothers to go to Galilee; there they will see me.'"

That's it. That's the familiar story, but listen to these familiar words again. "He is not here; he has risen just as He said. He has risen from the dead."

Friends, these words which are so familiar to you and me, *these words changed everything. These words rocked the universe. The world would never be the same again.*

Even time would be split into BC and AD, before Jesus Christ and after Jesus Christ.

Jesus Christ *had been dead*. He had not been asleep. He was not in a coma. He was *dead*. Then, God made him alive again.

And listen to this; this is important. The fact that God raised Him proves that what He claimed about Himself was true. It verified His claims, and what did He claim? He claimed to be the Son of God who came to heal the world, a process that is still ongoing today.

Now, this story which is at the very heart of the Christian message changes everything, and God has given us reminders, many reminders, of its truth.

First, this world-changing event is recorded for us in the Bible, and we cherish this written Word, don't we? But, most people around the world do not read this book. And, Jesus came to heal the *world*. He wants *everyone* to know this story, so He has left reminders that everyone can see.

He has left signs of LDBR (life, death, burial and resurrection) everywhere, even in our own lives. The most obvious is in nature, creation. We see a reflection of LDBR in the changing of the seasons. Trees are alive, green in summer. They lose their leaves and die, so to speak, in the fall. They are buried in the winter, and they are resurrected in the spring. We see this year after year. The *world* sees this year after year, a Hindu in India, a Buddhist in Nepal, an atheist in Germany. God loves them and us all and wants the world to know this story. Friend, I don't think it is a coincidence that we are surrounded in the natural world by a yearly replay of LDBR.

Have you ever noticed the cycles of LDBR in cultures and nations? We were just talking about the Roman empire under which Jesus was executed. We see this theme in the Roman Empire. That culture rose and lived. It began to decline and died. It was buried during the dark ages, and it was resurrected a thousand years later in the Italian renaissance. LDBR in a culture or nation.

How about our own lives? We see LDBR in our lives and in the lives of others all the way from the prodigal son in the Bible to your next door neighbor.

How about our physical lives? We are born, we live, we will age and die, and we believe we will be resurrected on the other side.

How about our spiritual journey, especially for those of us who came to faith as adults? We remember our old lives, then our old life died and was buried. We were resurrected in a new relationship with Jesus Christ.

We see LDBR in other places in our life stories. Perhaps you have lived through the life and death of a dream, or a hope, a relationship, a vocation. Then, that dream or relationship died, was buried and something new was raised up in its place.

These LDBRs don't happen just once in our lives, but over and over in many different ways. You may be walking through one of those places now.

So, we see LDBR in our physical lives, our spiritual journeys, relationships, families, dreams and hopes, life's work. LDBR seems to be the way God does things.

Now of course, we would love to skip the death and burial and proceed straight to the resurrection, but life doesn't work that way.

In John 12:24, Jesus said, "Unless a kernel of wheat falls to the ground and dies, it remains only a single seed. But, if it dies, it produces many seeds."

You see, before something is resurrected, something has to die, and dying hurts. At the time, we may think it's the end of the world, but friends, *there's more*, and this is great news!

Dying is not the end of the world. Dying is not the end of the world. Whether it is physical death, the death of a relationship or the death of a dream, it is a part of the journey, of your story. It is not the easy part, but it is not the end of the story.

And, do you know why it is not the end of the story? Because death, the last enemy, was defeated when God made Jesus of Nazareth alive again.

I Corinthians 15:55 says, "Death has been swallowed up in victory. Where, O death, is your victory? Where, O death, is your sting?"

The answer to that question is that death has no victory. The last enemy has been defeated.

Friends, the signs of LDBR are everywhere for the world to see. They are signs from a living God that He loves you, that death does not have the last word, that *there's more*.

We can live and rejoice knowing that we have been set free through the life, death, burial and resurrection of Jesus Christ.

He is risen, and that changes everything!

Rebecca Biegert Conti
New Britain, Connecticut
April 12, 2009

The Silent Measure

ADVENT MEDITATION

Saturday, December 20th, Morning
Titus 2:11-14

You and I inhabit a time in history that is defined by its context, by what has preceded and by what will follow. We live suspended, as it were, between Christ's first and second advents. An amazing space.

This reminds me of another breathtaking space which is also defined by its context. Each time we hear the "Hallelujah Chorus" in Handel's *Messiah,* we are suspended in the silent measure, filled with wonder as the tiny pause, conspicuously void of all sound, washes over us. We wait and can hardly bear the suspense until the final "Hallelujah!" breaks through the silence, leaving our hearts and eyes full.

But, what of the silence? Is the silent measure only a vacuum defined by the absence of notes? Ah, therein lies the beauty. Much more than the absence of sound, it is imbued with beauty and meaning because of its context. The space takes our breath away *because* of what has preceded and what will follow. Within the space itself, nothing is happening, and everything is happening.

As you walk through this particular day, I encourage you to ponder the notion of waiting. Wherever you find yourself and in whatever circumstance of waiting, I encourage you to dwell richly in that space. God is in it with you this day. May your silent spaces be filled with beauty and meaning.

Saturday, December 20th, Evening
Titus 2:11-14

As one whose vocation is, in part, to provide a place of rest and prayer for others, I have the opportunity to see the transformation of individuals as they are still. Most who arrive tired and discouraged, later leave refreshed and strengthened. Nothing is happening, and everything is happening in their stillness.

However, quiet waiting does not come easily to most of us. As Frederick Buechner writes, "We are none of us very good at silence. It says too much."

You and I wait for both the heavenly and the earthly, and the earthly waiting, accompanied by heartache, can bear down on us. As we wait for our Lord's return, our earthly concerns live side-by-side with our heavenly hope.

For what or for whom do you wait? Perhaps you have yet to make request of the Father. Perhaps you have already asked Him, and now...you...wait. Between the time you make the request and the time you begin to see His answer, you inhabit yet another amazing space. Nothing is happening while everything is happening.

Beloved, the Father has heard your request. He gives to you in the waiting and even as you sleep (Ps. 127:2). He is in this space with you, and His hand is on you and yours. One day the silent waiting will be broken with the "Hallelujah!" In the meantime, drink deeply.

"The Lord is in his holy temple; let all the earth be silent before him."
Habakkuk 2:20

Rebecca Biegert Conti
Flagstaff, Arizona
2008

God With Us, Always: Readying Ourselves for Advent, ed. By Stacey Gleddiesmith. Vancouver, British Columbia: Regent College Publishing, 2008, 40-41.

Acknowledgements

Thank you to my Flagstaff writing group: Mary K. Johnson, Stacey Wittig, Joyce Erfert, and Anne Childs. Your critiques and encouragement were invaluable to this new kid on the writing block (not to be confused with *writer's block*).

I am grateful to Janet Levin, my favorite let's-do-downtown-lunch friend, who regularly asked how the project was coming along, thus holding me accountable without even knowing it.

Thank you to Drs. Maxine Hancock and Loren Wilkinson of Regent College. Maxine, you introduced me to spiritual memoir as a genre, and Loren, your course introduced me to the wonder of the creative process.

I am grateful to Roberta Rogers who has painted every corner of northern Arizona and beyond. Thank you for your lovely rendition of my crooked tree.

Finally, thank you to Vincent whose idea it was for me to write this book. When you could have been writing music or playing the piano, you listened to my read-alouds. When my resolve weakened, you encouraged me to keep on keepin' on. And, your tech-savviness saved the day more than once. *Grazie mille. Sono pazzo di te.*

About the Author

Rebecca Biegert Conti holds a bachelor's degree in communications from the University of Texas and a master's degree in theology from Regent College. She speaks, teaches and leads retreats. She and her husband, Vincent, are the founders of Hidden Hollow Prayer Retreat near Flagstaff, Arizona.

Conti is the mother of four adult children and the grandmother of five. She enjoys reading, studying, the great outdoors and water fights. She is a terrible cook.

She and her husband live in Arizona and Connecticut.

www.CrookedTree.info

All profits from the sale of *Crooked Tree* will be donated to charity.

Made in the USA
Lexington, KY
21 March 2015